PERSPECTIVES IN READING NO. 6

CORRECTIVE READING
IN THE
HIGH SCHOOL CLASSROOM

Compiled and edited by

H. ALAN ROBINSON
University of Chicago
and
SIDNEY J. RAUCH
Hofstra University

Prepared by a Committee
of the
International Reading Association

BROTHER LEONARD COURTNEY, Publications Committee Chairman
H. ALAN ROBINSON, Conference Chairman

International Reading Association
Newark, Delaware 19711

1966

INTERNATIONAL READING ASSOCIATION

OFFICERS

1971 - 1972

President: THEODORE L. HARRIS, University of Puget Sound, Tacoma, Washington

President-Elect: WILLIAM K. DURR, Michigan State University, East Lansing, Michigan

Past President: DONALD L. CLELAND, University of Pittsburgh, Pittsburgh, Pennsylvania

DIRECTORS

Term expiring Spring 1972

THOMAS C. BARRETT, University of Wisconsin, Madison, Wisconsin

CONSTANCE M. McCULLOUGH, San Francisco State College, San Francisco, California

EILEEN E. SARGENT, Nicolet Union High School, Milwaukee, Wisconsin

Term expiring Spring 1973

MARJORIE S. JOHNSON, Temple University, Philadelphia, Pennsylvania

ROBERT KARLIN, Queens College, City University of New York, Flushing, New York

OLIVE S. NILES, State Department of Education, Hartford, Connecticut

Term expiring Spring 1974

WILLIAM ELLER, State University of New York, Buffalo, New York

WILLIAM J. IVERSON, Stanford University, Stanford, California

EUNICE SHAED NEWTON, Howard University, Washington, D.C.

*   *   *

Executive Secretary-Treasurer: RALPH C. STAIGER, University of Delaware, Newark, Delaware

Assistant Executive Secretary: RONALD W. MITCHELL, International Reading Association, Newark, Delaware

Publications Coordinator: FAYE R. BRANCA, International Reading Association, Newark, Delaware

*   *   *

Second printing February 1968
Third printing October 1971

ii

FOREWORD

CORRECTIVE READING IN THE HIGH SCHOOL CLASSROOM is the sixth in the Perspectives in Reading series. Previous Perspectives volumes have been concerned with *College-Adult Reading Instruction, Reading Instruction in Secondary Schools, Children, Books and Reading, Developing Study Skills in Secondary Schools,* and *First Grade Reading Programs.* A companion volume, *Corrective Reading in the Elementary Classroom,* the seventh Perspectives in Reading, will be published following the International Reading Association's Eleventh Annual Convention in May 1966, at which time the papers devoted to that subject will be given at the Perspectives Conference, May 4-5.

H. Alan Robinson and Sidney J. Rauch edited *Corrective Reading in the High School Classroom.* This volume includes the papers presented at IRA's Seventh Perspectives in Reading Conference which was held just prior to the annual meeting of the National Council of Teachers of English in Boston, November 23-24, 1965.

The International Reading Association is indebted to Dr. Robinson and Dr. Rauch for the care with which the conference was organized and the efficiency with which the papers were edited. IRA presents this volume with the hope that the ideas, methods, and techniques described will prove valuable to high school teachers in their continuing task of improving reading skills of high school students.

DOROTHY KENDALL BRACKEN
President, 1965-1966
International Reading Association

iii

CONTENTS

JERRY H. PARSLEY

LYONS TOWNSHIP HIGH SCHOOL, LAGRANGE, ILLINOIS

1. Promising Procedures in Corrective Reading: A Summary

TODAY's high school teacher often finds himself in a predicament as to how best to help a large number of students who are experiencing difficulty in his subject area. Often the teacher may suspect that the difficulty is somehow connected with the students' reading abilities. However, since the school's facilities for reading instruction may well be limited to assisting those students who have extreme reading problems and since the teacher himself may well have had no training in the teaching of reading, the teacher is at a loss in knowing what to do.

This *Perspectives in Reading* is designed especially for the teacher described in the preceding paragraph. The volume presents many procedures for improving instructions in the several content areas; procedures which are applications of various sound principles of reading. Not only are these procedures well founded, they are tangible and practical as well.

Some Principles and Procedures

In chapter two, Dr. H. Alan Robinson emphasizes that corrective reading instruction is the responsibility of all teachers who use the medium of print. Since reading is a process rather than a subject, it is impossible to separate reading from content; the practice of removing students from class for training with materials unrelated to academic subjects defeats the purpose of instruction. First, for many students there is little transfer of learning. Second, although some reading skills may be taught in one situation and applied in another, other skills need to be taught, applied, and reinforced specifically in each content area. The idea, then, that reading can be taught first and content later would seem to be fallacious; the improvement of reading ability should be part of the content area curriculum.

1

Teachers should be aware that a wide range of reading levels, strengths, and weaknesses exists in the content area classrooms, even in various "tracks." Included in this range are those students who are in need of corrective reading instruction. While these students are not as severely handicapped as the retarded readers—those who find reading a totally frustrating experience—they have various difficulties and deserve the maximum help which the content area teacher can give.

Among the general procedures for any content area teacher to use in the classroom are: *First,* the teacher should establish readiness for reading and studying to improve students' understanding. The teacher, therefore, should focus the students' attention on (1) relating prior experiences to reading and (2) developing key words and concepts necessary for various selections. *Second,* the teacher should assist students in developing and applying individual study techniques. Since "formula" study methods cannot be used mechanically in all content areas, application with necessary modifications should be stressed. *Third,* the teacher should utilize multi-level material whenever possible. Differentiated assignments offer increased opportunities for accomplishment by individual students. *Fourth,* the teacher should place emphasis on purposes for reading. These purposes for reading are innately linked with readiness for reading. *Fifth,* the teacher should be aware of the need for continuous evaluation as an integral part of instruction. Rather than evaluating an entire unit as such, the teacher should separate the work into smaller parts and evaluate the smaller parts. Finally, the teacher should develop classroom libraries in order to enrich students' backgrounds. These libraries should be relevant to each content area and should contain materials at various interest and reading levels. As an addition to existing school libraries, classroom libraries can provide on-the-spot motivation for reading.

Diagnostic Techniques

Dorothy Kendall Bracken stresses in chapter three that in today's high schools specific evaluations of student reading abilities are necessary. A teacher can no longer be satisfied with general comments; rather, evaluation in terms of specific areas of comprehension or specific vocabulary skills—to cite just two examples—is necessary.

In exploring the various factors that could contribute to reading difficulties which would require corrective instruction, the teacher could well employ a specialist approach. In this approach, a variety of measures, both formal and informal, may be used. The teacher, therefore, should weigh the relative values of standardized and informal testing, possibly using informal testing as a means of supporting or extending the results of standardized tests. Regardless of the measures used, it is important that the teacher evaluate expediently and assess accordingly.

An important area to be evaluated is that of mental capacity or ability. It is essential that the teacher be cautious of using just one capacity score as a valid measure. Further, since the capacity score may well be influenced by reading ability, the teacher should be cognizant that individual capacity tests administered by trained personnel often yield higher scores than group test scores.

Means of evaluating mental ability other than group or individual testing may be judiciously used: (1) speed of learning, (2) spoken vocabulary, (3) ability to organize ideas, (4) ability to see relationships among ideas, (5) ability to gain ideas from listening. In assessing the last-mentioned ability, two comparable tests may be used, one to be read by the student, and the other to be presented orally by the teacher.

Reading competency or reading level is a second important area to be evaluated. For this, the teacher may use the reading section of a battery of achievement tests. Much can be gained by the teacher's scoring these tests himself—or otherwise analyzing the student's errors—and by eliciting from the student the reasons why he responded in a certain way. Reading survey tests may also be advantageously utilized. Informal means of evaluating reading competency include: (1) standard informal inventories, (2) teacher-prepared informal inventories, and (3) checklists of skills.

The high school teacher should consider various other factors which can influence students' reading abilities. Among physical conditions which may be of significance are visual functioning, and a history of severe illness or unconsciousness. Emotional problems, educational problems such as class size or frequent change from school to school, and lack of interest or desire to learn must be considered in diagnosing reading difficulties.

The Reading Consultant

Nancy Vick, in chapter four, discusses the role of a reading consultant in content area classrooms. There are various services which the consultant can provide: (1) knowledge and understanding of students with reading problems, (2) assistance in applying the special study skills needed in each content area, (3) understanding of special methods of study, (4) demonstration of ways to teach vocabulary, (5) demonstration of ways to increase comprehension, and (6) help in selecting materials.

In assisting teachers to know and meet students on their own ground, the consultant can aid in checking reading levels, both instructional and independent. He may help identify those students who are in need of corrective reading. Further, the consultant may aid the teacher in understanding individual differences in motivation, interests, and mental ability.

To help classroom teachers with special study skills, the consultant may be of service in defining and separating the various skills so that they may be taught effectively. In ascertaining what study skills should be taught, consideration should be given to those necessary for locating information, for previewing and setting purposes for reading, for outlining, for note-taking, and for effectively using maps, charts, graphs, etc.

The consultant may introduce a special study method such as SQ3R to be used in specific content area classes.

Assistance in vocabulary may be given in several ways. First, the consultant may suggest methods by which words can be introduced. Second, he may suggest words which probably will give students difficulty. A third way the consultant can aid the teacher in the area of vocabulary development is to help him keep informed of appropriate standardized test results. Fourth, the consultant may suggest ways the teacher can give instruction in the efficient, intelligent use of the dictionary.

The consultant may provide additional behind-the-scene services: (1) aid in selecting, administering, and interpreting various tests; (2) aid in the use of informal means of evaluation; (3) assistance with teacher-made tests; and (4) assistance in developing instructional guides.

Reading and Writing

Leitha Paulsen and Nancy Larmer present in chapter five a method for using writing to help the poor reader. Since many prior attempts to integrate the reading and writing aspects of language arts have been futile, perhaps the difficulty has been in the traditional read-then-write approach. The method given in chapter five places first emphasis on writing. Through organizing his ideas, the student can better grasp the meaning of the writing of others. In addition, skills fixed in writing are more readily available for transfer to reading.

All good writing, it is assumed, has structure; good writing is not an amorphous mass of words but a harmoniously patterned whole. Since structure shapes meaning, the student must be made aware of structural unity. Further, the student should become conscious of structure in units of varying sizes and forms.

Employing the key word technique, the teacher assists the student in stripping down sentences which the student has written without guidance; then this skill is applied to the analysis of a paragraph. From the key word analysis, the main idea of the paragraph becomes apparent. The key word technique is thus used as a device for building structure into writing.

The student next formulates criteria for a good paragraph: a clearly stated main idea, all details supporting this main idea. In addition, he learns to limit the topic sentence. The student subsequently imposes structure on what others have written. The teacher leads the student through various paragraphs, showing that the main idea may be developed in several paragraphs. Thus, the student is better able to see the structure in the writing of others.

A second technique for dealing with paragraph unity is the use of carefully programed lessons which serve as cognitive "maps." These maps, patterned after samples of good paragraph writing, are worked out by the student and teacher. Maps for unity, order, and purpose are evolved; the student then follows these maps when writing paragraphs of his own. The maps not only show the student where to begin and where he wants to go, but also they prescribe each step to be taken.

Specificity is a second concept considered in chapter five. Students often tend to write in generalizations; their paragraphs lack "flesh and blood." In attempting to correct this weakness of student writing, teachers have frequently used the generalization: "Add more concrete details." The failure of this advice to significantly improve specificity suggests that teachers should otherwise aid students in being more concrete.

Seven methods of support are suggested in this chapter: (1) general to particular, (2) particular to general, (3) division or enumeration, (4) comparison and contrast, (5) details of space and time, (6) definition, and (7) cause-effect. The teacher should recognize, however, that paragraphs seldom contain but one method of support; more often methods of support are used in combination.

Evaluation of Author's Theme

Oliver Andresen emphasizes in chapter six that a significant purpose of reading literature is to gain insight into one's own problems. In order to assist students in ferreting out and passing judgment on the theme in a work of literature, it is valuable to utilize a profundity scale or measuring stick that can be used from story to story.

Such a profundity scale is detailed in this chapter. For the first plane of this scale, the physical plane, the reader is concerned only with the physical actions of the characters. At the mental plane, the concern is with both physical and mental actions. The third, or moral plane, involves physical and mental activities in light of a moral or ethical code relevant to time and place. The fourth plane, the psychological plane, incorporates the preceding levels plus the reasons why characters act as they do. The final plane of the profundity scale, the philosophical plane, embodies not only the preceding planes but also the universal quality—valid, but not entirely true—common to all man.

The teacher may devise and implement other scales for the teaching of literature. Such scales could be advantageously used in treating characterization, style, and the like.

Reading in the Social Studies

Marion Jenkinson observes in chapter seven that social studies embodies a wide range of content. The reading material that conveys social studies concepts is equally varied in terms of words, ideas, and modes of thinking. The student not only must bring meaning to the page, he also must derive meaning from it. To comprehend this material, the student needs the ability to interact appropriately with small and larger units, units which increase from single words through paragraphs. The student must first perceive words, then produce associations with these words. He must also select relevant associations and synthesize associations to produce meaning.

Two major considerations for increasing reading power in social studies, then, appear to be: (1) the development of functional word knowledge and (2) the development of strategies for understanding material of this content area. Three areas of functional word knowledge considered are (1) function words, (2) shifts of word meaning, and (3) classifying through word meaning.

The development of function words—coordinators or connectives— should be systematic, since these words give direction to thinking. Among these function words are those that indicate cause and effect (e.g., *because*), show condition (*if*), reveal contrast (*whereas*), indicate time relationships (*before*), and show parallel ideas (*therefore*). Further, among these words there are many which have varying meanings, for example, *while,* which may indicate time, condition, or parallel ideas.

Beginning with his own experience, the student should be made aware of the differences in meanings.

Difficulties which students in social studies experience with shifts of word meaning arise from the use of familiar words in unfamiliar contexts, and from the metaphorical implications of terms. Some understanding of students' difficulties may be gained from considering a term such as "machine age."

One of the main methods by which the social studies teacher can aid thinking through language is by using words to aid in the classification of ideas. Since most learning occurs in the recognition of similarities and differences, the teacher should explore the possibilities of direct classification through this method. Second, the teacher should recognize that the ability to apprehend overlapping classifications develops slowly and is barely achieved by the time a student enters high school.

The second major consideration for increasing reading power in social studies is the development of strategies for understanding material of this context area, and may be divided into teaching strategies and studying strategies. The first teaching strategy is development of awareness that the main idea of a passage may occur in various positions, or it may be implicit. A second teaching strategy is developing competence in comprehension through discussion with a student of his own errors.

Inherent disadvantages to the traditional method of outlining indicate that application of different methods of organization which follow the steps in the developing logic of children is an important strategy for studying. Two different methods, the hierarchical and matrix plan, are detailed in chapter seven.

Corrective Reading in Science

Students who need corrective reading instruction in high school science classes, George Mallinson observes in chapter eight, are primarily in "general" courses such as general science, general biology, or general physical science. These students, who often have been discouraged from taking more specialized courses, experience difficulty because the content of the general courses is drawn from many science disciplines, because extensive basic vocabulary is used and because many terms appear which are infrequently used in other materials. In addition, students often are taught by teachers who have received little or no training in the techniques involved in teaching reading or in the principles involved in learning to read.

Various positive actions—techniques which have been successfully tried—may be used by the science teacher to aid the student who needs corrective reading instruction. First, the teacher should take time to assist the reader, rather than merely asking him to read a certain number of pages. Second, the teacher should explain the various parts of the textbook e.g., table of contents, glossary, and index. A third positive action is having the students outline chapters of the textbook by copying and placing in the proper hierarchies the headings and subheadings. The student then places items in the correct hierarchies and explains his reasons for doing so. Fourth, the teacher can profitably use material other than the basic textbook. The use of this material should be carefully planned. Fifth, the science teacher can compare and explain varying usage of terms, for example, the scientific use of "energy" as compared with the everyday or colloquial use. Sixth, the teacher may have the student compare "science corners" of newspapers with appropriate sections of textbooks. Thus, the student is given the opportunity to detect errors, and he learns the importance of considering the authenticity of printed statements.

While there is no apparent panacea for the teacher of science working with students who require corrective reading instruction, judicious use of the foregoing positive actions—with adaptations when necessary—should help eliminate some of the problem reader's difficulties in science.

Corrective Reading in Mathematics

In chapter nine, Richard Muelder presents several methods for helping students read mathematics. The teacher should initially consider the use of various results of tests of mathematics skills which (1) help define the limits of the reading problem in this content area; (2) suggest categories of the problem, for example, speed in relation to comprehension; (3) focus attention on individual students' strengths and weaknesses; (4) point out the need for supplementary materials at a variety of levels; and (5) are useful in choosing aids to help promote readiness.

Various techniques for aiding students during the school year are detailed. By establishing, early in the year, purposes for reading mathematics and by suggesting ways for improving their reading, the teacher gives the students a good start. Ways of improving mathematics reading, suggested by Mr. Muelder, include, first, assisting students in using textbooks effectively; second, discussing the condensed nature of mathematical writing—the density of ideas, the importance of single words, and the high level of abstraction; third, emphasizing the need for several rates in reading mathematics; fourth, previewing an assignment to gain a general idea of what it is about; fifth, indicating the importance of careful rereading. For this rereading, the student may need to use pencil and paper, and work out parts to understand the whole. The student should try to picture what he is reading and should draw figures from definitions. He should also ask questions of the author and be critical. A sixth method is undertaking planned vocabulary study. The student may maintain his own glossary, not only for review of words but also for employing kinesthesia to aid learning.

Following presentation, these techniques should be evaluated by the students. This evaluation period offers the mathematics teacher an excellent opportunity to reemphasize the significance of efficient reading.

Questions Administrators Ask About Reading

Nila Banton Smith observes in chapter ten, as educational history goes, it is only recently that the teaching of reading has been considered an appropriate secondary-school subject. Administrators have only recently displayed a keen interest in the teaching of reading; they have shown an eagerness to do something worthwhile to improve reading instruction; they have actively sought information and advice.

A frequent question which administrators ask about reading in the secondary schools concerns the terminology which designates the differing types of reading instruction. For the purpose of this *Perspectives,* it is of value to distinguish between corrective and remedial reading. "Corrective reading," Dr. Smith states, "is used to designate the type of work done with less serious cases, those who perhaps are retarded only a year or so in terms of potential, who apparently have no deep-seated cause of difficulty, and who respond readily to treatment. Such students usually are taught in groups according to their particular needs and abilities."

A second question, frequently asked, concerns methods of convincing both students and parents that corrective reading instruction is necessary. The current job situation requires an education which is in a large part obtained from reading. Further, our modern, fast-moving civilization demands that everyone develop speedier and more effective reading skills. Since surveys reveal that many high school students are not reading as well as they should, corrective reading seems necessary.

A third question pertains the involvement of subject-matter teachers in corrective reading programs. Interest may be created by requesting teachers to be present at preliminary activities designed to create and encourage interest in the school's reading program. Teachers should be included in planning activities, too.

A fourth question concerns what specific things the content area teacher can do in his classroom. Chapters five through nine provide a wealth of valuable procedures.

Another frequent question, asked by administrators, pertains to locating qualified reading specialists. Placement bureaus and state educational institutions should be of help. Or, a school can develop a specialist from a member of its own ranks.

Answers to other questions—such as "What should I look for in employing a reading specialist?" "What may I expect of a reading consultant in secondary school?"—and pointers for starting a corrective reading program and for conducting in-service courses for teachers are given in detail in chapter ten.

H. ALAN ROBINSON

UNIVERSITY OF CHICAGO

2. Corrective Reading in the High School Classroom: Some Principles and Procedures

IN THE EARLY DAYS of American education, it was assumed that a student learned to read in the primary grades and then he read to learn in subsequent grades. Today we know that the assumption has little validity for the various disciplines present a multitude of differing, complex ideas on the printed page. In order to cope with the increasingly difficult concepts and the rapid-fire changes within a content field, many high school students need concrete assistance in understanding, interpreting, evaluating, organizing, and utilizing the required and supplemental reading demanded of them. The very curricular changes which demand heightened concept development, which call for the ability to deal with a variety of types of reading materials, and which put a premium on critical thinking, cause the reading tasks to magnify and extend the complexity of the reader's role.

The assistance needed by many of our students cannot be provided easily by someone else—other than the classroom teacher responsible for instruction in a particular content area. A reading teacher or reading consultant may be of some aid, but this person cannot possibly be as familiar with the types of reading in a given subject as the teacher-expert. And even if the reading specialist were particularly knowledgeable in a given field, the time the student normally needs the aid is when he is confronted with a problem within the classroom setting. Hence, any content area teacher who uses the medium of print as an instructional tool must accept the responsibility of helping his students contend efficiently and effectively with the reading tasks of the specific discipline.

Transfer of learning. In the past, educators seem to have depended on the questionable concept of transfer of learning to take care of the many

11

gaps they did not help their students fill during the high school years. For a large percentage of our high school students the gaps remained, for they could only make the transfer if the next learning situation was identical to the initial one. When the next learning situation displayed different characteristics, they faltered or failed because they did not possess the security or flexibility which would permit them to alter or amend the pattern initially established. To some extent, the problem still confronts us. When we introduce a reading skill in one framework, using a particular type of reading material, we often assume that it is taught and the student can now apply it in all other situations. Obviously, for many of our students, this is not valid. Direct guidance is needed in application and adjustment of specific skills as they are used with different materials and for different purposes.

If we agree that introduction, instruction, reinforcement, and review are essential aspects of learning, then it is conceivable that a skill may be introduced and taught in one situation, using certain kinds of materials; and reinforced in another situation, using other kinds of materials. Review is probably essential in both situations. But, if the skill is to be retained and used, it is best introduced and taught in the situation where it is immediately needed. For example, if the high school houses developmental reading classes (this is a slightly incongruous concept anyway, since there is no such subject as reading; the reading process depends upon a content), and if the "common" reading skills are introduced and taught in the reading classes, reinforcement and guided application are needed in the content areas that make use of such common skills. On the other hand, some skills (often specialized, but sometimes the common skills used in specific ways) are best introduced and initially taught when needed in a particular content area. The skill of outlining is far better taught initially with the expository material in social studies than with the narrative material of the literature class. The skill of following printed directions is needed far more frequently in mathematics, science, and home economics than in social studies, English or French.

Patterns of writing. One very important reason certain reading skills assume particular significance, in certain content areas, is because of differences in patterns of writing fundamental to specific disciplines. Smith (2) pointed out that although patterns in literature have been established for years, we have not looked carefully enough at the patterns in other subject areas. In her study of 206 textbooks used in grades seven through twelve, she found some distinct patterns in science, social studies, and mathematics. In science she named classification, explanation of a technical process, instructions for an experiment, detailed statement-of-facts, description of a problem-solving situation, and abbreviations and equations as the major patterns of writing. In social studies, she pointed out pictures and maps, cause and effect, sequential events with dates, comparison, detailed statement-of-facts, and propaganda as the most frequent patterns. In mathematics, she described the short paragraph setting forth a problem situation, explanation of a mathematical process, graphs and charts, and special symbols, signs and formulas as the chief patterns.

The content area teacher who is able to help poor readers view the most significant patterns and set purposes for reading in terms of the patterns, will probably help these students reap benefits they never felt were achievable. The recognition of pattern is the recognition of structure; many of the chapters in this book will promulgate the theme that problem readers can be helped to best remember and comprehend if they are able to use structure and organization to unearth ideas. For example, the student who becomes used to surveying his reading prior to study, searches not only for what the author says but how he says it. Recognition of a cause-effect pattern in social studies material will help the student set a purpose for reading and provide a pathway for ideas. Learning the characteristic pattern of most mathematical problems focuses the reader's concern on important steps leading to process as opposed to content. Hence, emphasis placed on the writing patterns in the various subject-matter areas will enhance reading skill, and will, in turn, improve the poor reader's opportunities of understanding and remembering the very ideas which are of chief concern to him and to his teacher.

Corrective Reading

Who is this poor reader capable of receiving help in the content area classroom? He is *not* the student with such severe learning difficulties and such a low reading level that he is totally unable to function in the classroom. He is *not* the student with a very low reading level who has a severe emotional problem. He *is* the student who is not reading up to his capacity; who usually understands and retains what he hears but has recognizable problems in handling the textbooks, reference materials, and supplementary reading required in the particular content area classroom. In the next chapter, Mrs. Bracken suggests some concrete methods of identifying the student in need of corrective help, and also indicates specific ways of learning more about his individual strengths and weaknesses.

In the concluding chapter Dr. Smith contrasts corrective reading and remedial reading in an endeavor to enlighten the administrator. She makes a valuable distinction and one which the content area teacher must keep in mind. The severely retarded reader in need of remedial help needs highly individual help based on highly specialized diagnosis. The content area teacher cannot be expected to provide such treatment. The learner in need of corrective reading, on the other hand, is not severely retarded in reading and usually responds well to treatment. Such treatment is not only within the realm of possibility for the content area teacher, but actually his responsibility. This entire book focuses on underlying principles and pragmatic activities related to that responsibility.

Here are some examples of high school students who could profit from corrective help in reading:

(1) John Jeffrey is a high school senior who obtains satisfactory grades but never seems to have time for anything else but study. He belongs to no clubs and doesn't participate in any other school activities. His intelligence is high and he scores extremely high on a reading achievement test. On questioning, John indicates that he spends six to eight hours every day on his school work. He finds it necessary to read over and over his materials in order to remember the information and concepts. His normal study technique is memorization.

John appears to need help in learning an organized attack on his reading in addition to learning how to make notes and outline. Although his reading level is high, the study reading he accomplishes takes its toll on him by shutting out many other life activities. John needs help from every teacher in how to most efficiently deal with the various reading materials in the particular disciplines.

(2) Jacqueline Crisp just passes in all of her tenth grade subjects involving reading, although the results of intelligence tests and her general alert attitude would suggest that she should do mush better. She reads haltingly when called on to read orally. Her written assignments based on outside reading seem to show that she uses words incorrectly quite often. She does poorly on the vocabulary section of reading achievement tests.

Jacqueline seems to need help in vocabulary development in all of her subjects. Perhaps the English teacher might help her work out a method of improving her vocabulary, but obviously the teachers in each subject will need to help her deal with the technical vocabulary of the particular area.

(3) Mike Robbins is having a terrible time in ninth grade General Science. He does well enough in his other subjects but he seems to be quickly moving toward the failure level in this subject. Upon examination of the General Science textbook, which is the one book being used in the course, the reading level is approximately at grade fourteen. Mike's reading level is about grade ten.

Since the textbook will not be discarded, Mike needs to be helped in learning how to make use of the various contextual, typographical, and structural aids in the book. He needs to learn a study system using the book. This, of course, can best be accomplished by the science teacher and Mike rather than someone not familiar with the book or the subject. (Incidentally, the classroom teacher will want to soon determine whether or not it is wise to use this particular textbook.)

Here is an example of a high school student who could profit from remedial help working with a trained specialist rather than expecting appreciable help from the classroom teacher:

Bert Cluny is unable to read any of the materials normally used for instructional purposes in any of his classes. He finds it difficult to communicate ideas even when material is read to him. He achieves, on a standardized reading test, four grades below his grade level and six grades below his very fine potential. He seems nervous and distracted in all of his classes except physical education.

Bert must obviously have a more intensive diagnosis, but just from the evidence at hand he appears to be in need of remedial reading and perhaps other kinds of assistance too. The classroom teacher cannot do more than be sympathetic, try to make learning as attainable as possible under the circumstances, and give full cooperation to a specialist who should be working with Bert. In the event that no such specialist is available, the teacher should attempt to get help from an outside agency.

The examples cited above are but a few of the many types of possible problems. Examples, unfortunately, can often mislead because of too much specificity or too much generalization. These are just meant to serve as pragmatic definers of the terms used—corrective or remedial reading.

Track systems and other methods of school-wide grouping will not eliminate the need for corrective reading. The range of reading levels may be more limited in the classroom when the school has used a grouping system based on reading achievement, but the individual strengths and weaknesses of the individuals in the classroom remain varied and multitudinous. The high school teacher in the classroom using the content of the discipline becomes a corrective reading specialist in his particular subject area.

Principles and Procedures

In chapter one, Mr. Parsley summarized a number of basic principles and procedures suggested by the authors of various chapters in this book. He cited several general procedures suggested in this chapter for the use of all content area teachers. These procedure-principles are elaborated upon here along with additional recommendations of a general nature. Chapters five through nine, concerned with the various subject matter fields, specify application of these suggestions and add new ones pertinent to particular disciplines.

1. *Readiness.* The problem reader needs special emphasis placed on readiness for a given content and for the use of certain skills that he must be prepared to use in order to read and study that content. Time spent on developing readiness with those who need it will prove profitable for both students and teacher. It is not time taken away from teaching the subject matter; it is the wise use of time which will result in improved understanding and retention of ideas on the part of the student who has been experiencing difficulty with reading assignments.

Whether the reading assignment is to be accomplished in class or at home, the teacher must set aside enough time prior to the reading for the development of readiness. Readiness might normally consist of (a) relating the past experiences of the students to the new reading assignment, (b) discussing technical vocabulary, (c) setting a purpose(s) for the reading. The use of earlier reading assignments and other vicarious experiences, as well as actual experiences when pertinent and possible, as a tool to opening a new door is almost always beneficial. The student realizes that he is not approaching an assignment completely foreign to him. Discussions of a few significant words or terms used in the assignment, prior to reading it, also help students feel a sense of familiarity when they approach their assignments. Discussion of technical vocabulary, in addition, aids in setting a purpose or purposes for the reading since the reader is urged to find out more about the contexts surrounding the words. Good questions by the teacher and questions elicited from class members can also be used to set purpose(s).

The type of readiness activity described above is probably important for every student. It is, however, particularly significant for the reader who finds the assignment difficult. Some of his insecurity and his fear of the complex and unknown is diminished. He knows a little something at least about what he is to read before he reads it. Setting purpose(s) has limited his responsibility and he isn't responsible for remembering that mass of black print.

Organizationally, the teacher may work on such readiness activities with the whole class, a group, or an individual. The assignment, a more complex assignment, or another activity may be given to those students not engaged with the teacher in preparing for the reading assignment. In most instances readiness work can be accomplished within a ten minute period.

2. *Study techniques*. Readiness for reading and study is an important concept but may have limited usefulness, unless the student has developed study techniques which will enable him to organize, and, hence, comprehend and retain, the information and ideas he meets on the pages of print. The content area teacher must play a role in helping the student, especially the problem reader, develop such techniques. Each discipline organizes and presents ideas in different ways. Each piece of reading matter has a somewhat different pattern than the next.

In each subject matter classroom where reading plays a vital role, the teacher should direct orientation and follow-up lessons on approaches to study with the important reading materials which will be utilized frequently. Students need practice in overviewing or surveying or previewing the material they are to study before engaging in the study act. Time given to this activity in class, particularly at the beginning of the year and when new materials are introduced, will help the student develop the technique for his independent reading.

Students can be helped to examine their own study techniques and make efforts to improve them if teachers in the particular content fields· will talk over each student's techniques with him, individually. There is no one technique that is best for all students nor should a teacher be attracted to a particular study method and enforce its use upon all students. Overall, the student needs guidance in learning how to survey, prior to study; to set up reading purposes, to make organized notes, and to review his efforts.

The study of a science chapter in a science textbook with its experiments, with its diagrams and accompanying text, and with its rather terse expository style is not quite the same activity as the study of a social studies chapter with its maps and charts, its greater redundancy in presentation of words and ideas, and its somewhat more narrative style.

Obviously, the student who learns how to study a chapter, any chapter, will relate some of his knowledge to all chapters. The problem reader, as pointed out previously, tends to have great difficulty transferring such knowledge from one reading situation to another. The teacher must help him learn how to contend with the specific materials in the specific content area.

3. *Multi-level materials.* With the birth of paperbacks and other means of packaging printed materials, accompanied by important changes in school curriculums in the content areas, it is almost impossible for the teacher to avoid the use of multi-level materials even if he wanted to do so. A planned program using multi-level materials, when possible written at the instructional reading levels of the problem readers in particular, will permit them to contribute to class discussions and begin to make them more effective in reading. There are materials available today at many reading levels dealing with most of the concepts important in each content area.

If the teacher expects students to do a great deal of independent work through textbook assignments, it is desirable that several reading levels be represented. One way of assuring this is for a subject matter department to order a copy or two of a textbook designated for a specific grade level or course from each of the publishers they feel have adequate to excellent books. These books ought to be evaluated on the basis of strength in subject matter and ranked in 1-2-3 order. Then a readability formula (*1*) ought to be applied to each text. In ordering the books, both strength in subject matter and readability should be considered. The teacher might want to order three textbooks and assign the most difficult to the readers who appear to be superior, the grade level book to the average readers, and, if there is an easy edition, the easiest to the poorest readers. Even though every bit of information may not be contained in each book, ideas can be shared by discussion and interchange of books. In fact, critical reading becomes a daily occurrence.

4. *Differentiated assignments.* Another way of helping the learner with a reading problem is to be sure that his assignments are feasible. Poor readers are often frustrated at the outset when they face a large mass of black print with hazy purposes for reading or perhaps none at all other than, "Read chapter six and come to class prepared to talk about it." They may also be very dismayed when confronted with too many questions to answer (purposes of reading), or questions that call for evaluations beyond their abilities.

Whether using one textbook or multi-level materials, the teacher may ask different individuals to be responsible for different assignments. Such attention to individual abilities enhances discussions, and enables various individuals to contribute in depth on specific topics. The ability to listen becomes a significant asset because each "reporter" has carefully read only a part of the total chapter or selection in terms of his own purposes.

5. *Questioning.* An obvious tool for the teacher, apparent as a part of each of the preceding points, is the art of questioning. The teacher who carefully thinks through questions to ask during the readiness period can help the poor reader immeasurably. Questions which may be turned into purposes for reading have immediate value. The more guidance students receive through the questions devised by the teacher, the more opportunity they will have to emulate the examples set as they preview or survey the material they are to study on their own.

The teacher can also help the poor reader feel an important part of the group by directing questions toward him which he is likely to be able to answer. In some cases the teacher may want to meet with a small group of poor readers by themselves before a total class discussion to assist them in organizing their thoughts and to help clarify some confusing areas. Questions asked of the poor reader should not be limited to the literal comprehension type—*What? When? Where? Who? How?* Poor readers are perfectly capable of coping with *Why?*, if they have received prior help with skills of interpretation with materials at levels commensurate with their reading abilities.

6. *Evaluation.* Poor readers, especially, must be able to meet with frequent success. They often meet with exceptionally infrequent success for evaluations of their progress most often come in the form of tests of large units of work. There is more opportunity for successful experiences, if small units of work are evaluated by the teacher and by the student. Self-evaluation of smaller units of work will permit the poor reader to accept failures which can be turned into successes in the near future rather than having to wait for the results of a big test.

Obviously, the evaluation of small units does not negate the evaluation of large units of work. The poor reader, however, is much better able to cope with the large unit test if he has viewed, analyzed, and reviewed the smaller units. Continuous evaluation as a part of the total teaching pattern can make a vital contribution to the reading progress of the poor reader *(4)*.

7. *Classroom libraries.* Poor readers in a content area often have

limited background experiences related to the area. They find it difficult to gain these experiences at a rapid enough pace working with the materials being used for instruction. One way of helping poor readers fill in on this background and have them enjoy doing it is to have a classroom library. The math class, the science class, the physical education class, the industrial arts class should all contain some type of classroom library that changes at least once a month. The materials in it should be related to the subject area and sometimes to particular units of work. The materials should range in reading level from the lowest to the highest reading level represented in the class. Some of the books and magazines should be non-fiction and others fiction. All will help enrich backgrounds, and increase the ability of poor readers to make contributions.

Classroom libraries are necessary whether a school has a central library or not; more so, of course, if there is no central library. Teachers cannot bemoan the fact that students do not do enough "outside reading" when the books are not accessible at all times and when the teachers are not actively encouraging students to read. Obviously, too, the school librarian cannot be left with the total task, nor can the English teacher who has no more responsibility for this than the geometry teacher, the history teacher, the biology teacher. Each teacher in the school has the obligation of helping poor readers widen their backgrounds in his subject area, just as each has the obligation for helping with skill development. In this area of "free" reading there are probably more teachers with obligations. The physical education teacher, the art teacher, the music teacher—and others who may not rely on written material for direct instruction most of the time—certainly can house small classroom libraries and encourage students to broaden their backgrounds in their particular areas.

8. *Non-print materials.* Although poor readers need as much aid as possible with reading skills, they also need to be encouraged to turn to reading; the content area teacher can help through the use of non-print materials. The poor reader must be able to learn through a variety of other media planned to reinforce and to replace reading. Tapes, records, filmstrips, films, TV, models, and realistic experiences are useful if they are selected, evaluated, and utilized as carefully as print materials. They can be potent aids or useless time consumers.

Often a well-selected filmstrip can clarify a concept that the poor reader found very hazy when he was reading the assigned selection. The poor reader must be as carefully prepared for the filmstrip, however, as he was for the reading selection. Time spent in linking his background experience to the film strip presentation, discussing technical vocabulary, and setting purpose(s) for the viewing will add to understanding and retention.

9. *Classroom organization.* The poor reader can be helped by the content area teacher through the use of many whole group techniques, but eventually the teacher must work with him in a small group situation or individually. Although it is difficult to group in class periods that range usually from 42 to 48 minutes, there are too many individual needs in any given classroom to permit lack of some individualization of instruction. The content area teacher must plan at times to work with certain small groups or specific individuals while the other members of the class work on other assignments.

For the teacher who is not used to grouping but wants to do so in order to care for some individual needs, here is one suggestion. Start by using one period a week for homework assignments to be done in class. Make sure the assignments are differentiated so that no student will be done before the class period is over. Those who don't finish assignments may do so at home. Observe the way your students study the first time you try the method. Give help to individuals as you walk around the room. Gradually, on another day, work for longer periods with individuals in need of your help. Then one day, after spotting a common need among five or six of your students, work with one small group for twenty minutes or so. Remember your students will need to become comfortable with the method just as you will. As long as you have given assignments to those you are not working with that will carry them through the period, and as students really see the value of the method, it will become a valuable part of each week's work. Eventually, you may want to group more frequently, or in different ways for different things.

10. *Team teaching.* Cooperative planning and cooperative teaching appear to hold much promise for the poor reader in the secondary school classroom. Corrective instruction in reading the material of a particular content area could be planned into the teaching design and implemented rather easily when two or more teachers are on the scene. It would even be possible for the reading teacher or reading consultant (if the school has one) to act as a team teacher, if the activities were carefully and cooperatively planned. Such a team effort allows the corrective reading to take place in the content area classroom and directed by a specialist. The classroom teacher may learn some reading techniques and the reading specialist will certainly learn about the content area. Most important of all, the poor readers should derive maximum benefit.

Concluding Remarks

Students in need of corrective reading will always be present in our classrooms. No matter how well students are taught to read the materials present in the elementary school, a large number of them will meet complex materials, too difficult for them to cope with, when they arrive on the scene in the secondary school. Others will come from the elementary school with low reading levels because the pace was too fast for them, or because their experiential backgrounds were poverty-stricken, or because they were the victims of a multitude of inhibiting factors. Some will read well in certain types of materials, but not in others. No matter the reason, they will be present. Teachers will need to be prepared to work with them.

When possible, content area teachers in secondary schools will want to take a reading course which will provide them with many techniques to use in helping the poor reader. They will want to work with reading specialists who may be available in their school systems. They will also want to read current professional material from which they may extract ideas. It is hoped that this book will offer enough in the way of specific suggestions to provide some fundamental assistance.

REFERENCES

1. Dale, Edgar, and Chall, Jeanne S., "A Formula for Predicting Readability," *Educational Research Bulletin,* Ohio State University, Vol. 27, pp. 11-20, 28, 37-54.
2. Smith, Nila Banton, "Patterns of Writing in Different Subject Areas—Part I," *Journal of Reading,* 8 (October 1964), 31-37.
3. Smith, Nila Banton, "Patterns of Writing in Different Subject Areas—Part II," *Journal of Reading,* 8 (November 1964), 97-102.
4. Strang, Ruth, *Diagnostic Teaching of Reading.* New York: McGraw-Hill Book Co., 1964.

DOROTHY KENDALL BRACKEN

SOUTHERN METHODIST UNIVERSITY

3. Diagnostic Techniques for Classroom Use

D ISCUSSIONS with high school teachers often begin with the question, "What trends in the reading field do you see in relation to diagnosis?" Discovering the strengths and weaknesses of teen-age readers is a vital issue in the improvement of reading instruction. No longer can a teacher smugly say, "This student's comprehension is poor, his speed slow, word attack unsatisfactory." Which *areas* of comprehension? What degree of *efficiency* in speed? Which word-attack skills? Furthermore what is "poor" and "slow" and "unsatisfactory"? With whom is the student being compared? Is his capacity for learning taken into consideration? What attention has been given to physical, emotional, and environmental factors? These and similar questions need to be raised whenever there is a discussion of poor reading performance. In order for high school teachers to work effectively with students, they need to consider the reading specialist's approach to diagnosis, to the place of standardized tests, to the role of informal testing, to the advantages of observation as a diagnosis, to the place of standardized tests, to the role of informal testing, to the advantages of observation as a diagnostic tool, to the teaching-learning situation as a valid test situation, and to the task of synthesizing these various ways of securing pertinent information.

A special reading teacher is usually highly successful in helping students with reading difficulties because the teaching approach is diagnostically oriented. Rather than an attitude of "Here I am to give you content material (or teach you a skill) and then test you on it to see if you learned it," the specialist's approach to the student is, "We'll find out everything we can about the factors which operate in this learning situation and give help at the points of weakness as we are able to discover them." The former is a teach-test (sometimes teach-test-punish!) approach, while the latter is a diagnose-plan-remediate line of action. Classroom teachers can readily see that the latter attitude makes possible

23

a contribution from the learner, thus building within him an attitude of seeking to understand his difficulty and of helping to find ways to overcome it.

In proceeding with diagnostic techniques in the classroom, the teacher must consider the role of standardized tests in relation to informal tests. The trend is to realistically appraise what the scores on standardized tests indicate and to better interpret tests results. Certainly we should not abandon the valuable tool of the standardized test merely because of our misuse of the information it yields. On the other hand, enthusiasm for informal methods of testing points a way for all teachers, regardless of availability of standardized tests and measures. Informal tests also provide ways of substantiating results secured from the more formal standardized tests. Arthur McDonald wrote (12):

> Modern appraisal, however, depends on more than just the administration and interpretation of standardized reading tests. Appraisal, as here used, means the assessment and analysis of the status of reading performance based on definite expert judgment. Thus, an appraisal of a pupil or a class will be based on all means of securing information which are appropriate to the situation and which are congruent with the law of parsimony. So, in appraising reading performance of a class, a teacher will resort to a wide range of means of securing information, including standardized tests, informal reading surveys, planned observation of pupil behavior in reading situations and other behavioral settings, study of relevant background data, etc.

Master teachers have always used observation as a means of studying their students, but today an even greater emphasis is being placed on the informal use of observing the student as an important means of diagnosing his strengths and weaknesses. To go further, the teaching-learning situation itself presents an opportunity for the teacher to gather diagnostic data concerning students' reading performance. At the University of Chicago Reading Conference, Mary Austin (15) stated:

> Diagnosis is an on-going activity in the classroom of an able teacher who regards teaching as a continuous diagnostic process—a daily evaluation of children's needs as they learn. The skilled teacher sees diagnosis as a first step in planning appropriate instruction and materials for his students.

Today's teacher must use all the techniques available in order to evaluate expediently and assess accurately the wide range of performance found in the average high school classroom. Therefore, he needs to know

(1) the techniques for discovering mental ability, in order to set up expectancies for his students; (2) techniques for discovering reading competencies so that he can give help in areas of weaknesses; and (3) considerations which must be made of other pertinent factors, since many students may have deficiencies resulting from problems in hearing, vision, emotion, environment, motivation, or interest.

Techniques for Discovering Mental Ability

One formal way of securing an indication of native capacity of students is, of course, to administer a standardized group intelligence test, such as the California Test of Mental Maturity (4), the Primary Mental Abilities Test (14) or similar tests suggested by Austin, Bush, and Huebner (1). Since most schools have a testing program which includes the administration of mental ability tests, the scores from such tests are often available from cumulative cards.

Several warnings should be considered at this point. First, attention is called to the fact that when the scores on *group* intelligence tests are compared with those on *individual* intelligence tests given by a trained psychologist for the same student, the *individual* test often yields a higher score than the *group* test. Second, teachers and administrators must remember that the score on a mental maturity test *is not the pupil's I.Q.* but only represents a score the student made on that *particular test* on that *particular day* in the student's life. Furthermore, any score is subject to the physical stamina and emotional status of the student *at that moment;* hence it is important to consider mental maturity tests as *indications* of capacity rather than *as* capacity. Third, important also is to consider the amount of reading involved in the test and the unfairness of this characteristic of the test to those having difficulty with reading. Fourth, it is well to think of a test score as just that—*one* test score—and not some infallible number to be held forever in "holy esteem." And, finally, since mental maturity scores are subject to all of the above named extenuating circumstances, they should be handled as highly confidential data.

For all practical purposes, a teacher can rank student capacity expectancies as normal, below, or above. However, even this general information on capacity should be carefully guarded for fear of damaging or prejudging a student's educational future. Many teachers code information on student capacity when placing it in their record books.

If a teacher has recorded a standardized test score—or better yet, test scores, accumulated over a period of years, which indicate something of the capacity of the student—informal observation may serve to either reinforce or change the indication of capacity. Or, if no test scores are available, informal observation can supply information useful to the teacher as he attempts to reach a tentative conclusion relative to each student's capacity.

Strang often has pointed out that if the teacher observes students in the following four ways he will have some indication of that pupil's learning power: (1) speed of learning, (2) speaking vocabulary, (3) organizing ideas, and (4) seeing relationship of ideas. A teacher might list the names of his students down the left side of a sheet in his progress book and, across the top, place the items suggested by Strang. This type of observation will extend throughout many assignments as a teacher directs learning situations. Using a check system, the teacher can record which students appear to learn with the greatest speed, which students take an average amount of time, and which ones are slow in completing assignments.

Since oral language activities are part of almost every lesson, the teacher has many opportunities to observe and record fluency in oral language. Is this student having difficulty expressing his thoughts? Is this one exceptional in the extent of his vocabulary, complexity of sentence structure, or effectiveness of communication? Do others move satisfactorily in the language arts area?

Observing and recording as students organize ideas is the third way a teacher can determine something about students' native ability. A simple classification assignment may be given the students, such as: "Classify into four categories all the words (or phrases or sentences) in the following list." Giving several classification assignments, each progressively more difficult than the last, is one method teachers can use in assessing the capacity of students. Seeing relationship between ideas, an activity closely related to organizing ideas, is another activity in which a teacher can observe students' abilities. Asking students to determine the ways a list of phrases relate to one another, when some represent the main ideas of a paragraph and others simply name details, is a way of observing which students recognized relationships. Several exercises of this type, increasing in difficulty, yield important information for the teacher.

No one of these informal tests alone is completely valid for indicating capacity. However, a combination of observations based on several types of performance will enable a teacher to set up expectancies of accomplishment for his students after other inhibiting factors related to reading problems have been reviewed.

Another way to informally secure an indication of capacity is to use listening ability as a measure. Years ago, Durrell and Sullivan produced a reading capacity test (6) for the elementary level which was made up of selections read to the children after which they responded to questions. Any high school teacher can readily devise an informal listening test based on this idea, using material at hand plus questions he creates for the selection. Or, the second form of a reading comprehension test can be read orally to a class and each student respond to the questions in writing. Betts's (2) capacity level represents the high level of reading at which a student is able to achieve 75 per cent comprehension or better when listening to someone read. Harris (8) recommended the selection of ". . . a reading test that measures level of comprehension and has at least two equivalent forms. One form is given to the child in the usual way. In giving the other form the test is read to the child as slowly as is necessary, and his spoken answers are recorded. The test used should be one in which speed is of little importance."

Techniques for Discovering Reading Competencies

Important competencies in reading achievement include reading level, types of comprehension, and word-attack skills. How to determine reading level has been a topic of much discussion during the past few years. While it is true that determining reading levels is a complex problem, it is also true that any classroom teacher who is sincerely interested in determining the approximate reading level of each pupil may do so through both formal and informal means.

In considering the formal ways, several types of standardized tests may be administered: the reading section of a battery of achievement tests, tests which accompany basal reading series, or survey reading tests.

The least information probably comes from the reading section of a general achievement battery. On the other hand, if the reading section of such a battery provides sub-test scores, information from this source can be helpful in indicating reading level. If the total score and the sub-scores on the reading section are available to teachers, these may serve as the formal indication of reading level, in addition to some information on comprehension, vocabulary, and speed, since these areas represent the usual breakdown of reading performance in standardized reading tests. However, much more valuable to the teacher are the actual test papers, since a study of mistakes made on tests is a diagnostic technique profitable for both teacher and pupil.

Tests which accompany basal reading programs usually include grades seven and eight and offer a great deal of diagnostic information. If the use of the basal reading series is continued through the seventh and eighth grades—as a number of reading specialists urge—and if teachers at these levels have the tests which accompany the basal series, they have a valuable means for securing diagnostic information as the result of administering such tests.

Standardized survey tests—such as the Gates Reading Survey Tests (7), the Iowa Silent Reading Tests (9), or the Diagnostic Reading Test [Survey Section] (5)—are appropriate for use at the high school level. The Gates test is devised for use in grades three through ten. While the Iowa Silent Reading Test is recommended for grades nine through thirteen, the Diagnostic Reading Test (Survey Section) is satisfactory for grades seven through thirteen. Subtest scores yield information on comprehension, vocabulary, and speed; raw scores on these tests are convertible to percentile ranks, or grade levels, or both. Remembering that total scores often represent the point at which the student breaks down (his frustration level) the teacher will use reading materials for informal testing—and later for instruction—at a *lower* level than that which is actually indicated on a standardized test.

Although they do not exemplify standardized tests, Niles, Bracken, Dougherty, and Kinder (13) have devised diagnostic tests to be administered to ninth and tenth grade classes. The items covered in the ninth grade test are: words (sound, context, dictionary, structure, syllabication, word families); and sentences and ideas (paragraphs, inference, sequences). The tenth grade test includes: words (context, structure, sound, dictionary); figurative language; sentence meaning; judgments; inferences; relationships; and imagery. The tests reveal the area of each student's weakness and practice exercises are provided to correct those weaknesses.

As for informal ways to diagnose, Nila Banton Smith (17) reports that from an historical point of view, during the years between 1935 and 1950, "the use of informal diagnosis with basal readers was an innovation." Betts was first to describe this technique in his discussion of "The Informal Inventory" appearing in the first edition (1946) of *Foundations of Reading Instruction,* pages 443-481.

Because the informal reading inventory yields a fairly accurate instructional reading level, in addition to many other items useful in subsequent teaching (such as independent and frustration levels), it is highly regarded today as a realistic and practical way of evaluating a student's ability to handle print. Not only will it yield an approximate reading grade level, but also it pinpoints specific needs of the reader.

Some excellent informal inventories have been commercially produced most of which, however, are appropriate, for the lower grades. From a study of Smith's (*18*) *Graded Selections For Informal Reading Diagnosis, Grades Four Through Six,* a high school teacher could quite easily construct his own inventory. The procedure on the informal inventory is based on a diagnostic use of oral reading. The pupil reads aloud a passage which the instructor is reasonably sure is easy for him. The initial reading is followed by oral reading of other selections each more difficult than the last. The reader is asked literal comprehension questions and interpretation questions; vocabulary is checked from the point of view of sight words, phonetic analysis, and structural analysis. The Spache Diagnostic Reading Scales (*20*) "are a series of integrated tests, carefully developed over a period of eight years to provide standardized evaluations of oral and silent reading skills and of auditory comprehension. The tests are individually administered, and may be used to determine the proficiency of normal and retarded readers at elementary school levels and of retarded readers in junior and senior high school age groups."

The teacher must be a perceptive observer if the informal inventory is to serve its maximum purpose. In other words, the teacher must know what he is listening for and how to evaluate what he hears. Listening to someone read orally is one thing; listening to record, in order to interpret a pupil's strengths and weaknesses, requires perceptive listening.

High school teachers would have little difficulty constructing factual and interpretative questions to determine a pupil's comprehension in these two areas. Using oral reading to determine, diagnostically, the needs of the reader in the area of sight vocabulary or word recognition is more difficult.

First of all, the teacher must note carefully and record the words which are not recognized instantly; these represent the deficiencies in sight vocabulary. Next, he must notice the pupil's use of structural analysis as he attempts to work out words for himself. Does he recognize compound words as two small words joined together? Does he see affix words in the light of roots, prefixes, and suffixes? Is he able to look at a word and tell how many syllables it will probably have? Can he then proceed to divide it into syllables according to the simple formula VCCV or VCV (V= vowel, C=consonant)? Thirdly, the teacher observes the reader's use of phonetic analysis, recording carefully whether the student is able to recognize consonant sounds, vowel sounds, consonants and vowels in various combinations, etc.

The teacher should also observe the reader's ability to blend the phonetic elements, since the ability to blend is a higher level of performance than mere "calling" the sounds. The blending ability is essential to "unlocking" the word, since blending the sounds according to structural and phonetic knowledge is really "saying the word in slow motion."

Careful details for administering the reading inventory are presented by Johnson and Kress (10) in one of the Reading Aids bulletins, published by the International Reading Association, entitled *Informal Reading Inventories*. These two experts show the teacher the underlying concepts of an informal inventory, the procedures to use in dealing with an individual inventory, those to be used with a group inventory, how to prepare the materials, and how to score and record the results. In their conclusion, Johnson and Kress voice the importance of the teacher constructing his own inventory:

> Far greater impact on both diagnostic and instructional work is apt to be felt when *construction* of inventories, not merely *administration* of them, is experienced. Whenever possible, of course, building, administering, and interpreting an inventory should be done under the supervision of someone well versed in techniques for informal evaluation. In this way, one's individual limitations could be more readily overcome. However, even when such expert guidance is not available, much can be learned through successive experiences with one's own inventory materials. Careful selection and preparation of materials, followed by try-outs of the inventory with children and resultant modifications, should be real learning experiences.

Another source of invaluable help is the very comprehensive "Checklist Record of Classroom Observations of Pupil's Reading" which appears in Strang's definitive book, *Diagnostic Teaching of Reading* (23). The checklist is divided into the following parts: I. When Giving Oral Reports II. Oral Reading and Group Instruction Periods III. Dramatization of Stories IV. Silent Reading Situation (Free-choice Reading or Library Time) V. Listening to Story Read Aloud.

One teacher who devised his own individual inventory proceeded in the following way: (1) He made a form for his entire class on which to record the areas he needed to consider. (2) From permanent cumulative record cards he secured data pertinent to his aim. (3) He made a separate chart for each member of his class, listing in *detail* the items he needed to observe. (4) He chose five reading selections which represented five reading levels, his own grade with two levels above and two levels below. (5) He constructed comprehension questions, varying from main idea questions to inference questions, a set each for the five separate pieces of materials. (6) Then he planned his lessons for several days so that the class would be involved in some educationally worthwhile activity, thus enabling him to hear each student read orally to him one at a time without disturbing the others in the class. By taking four students before school and four after school hours, this teacher, in one week's time, has accomplished his aim of hearing each individual read orally and had accumulated information on each which was invaluable for making lesson plans throughout the remainder of the term. "I did not lose a week," he commented. "Quite the opposite. I gained a semester!"

The diagnostic information which he accumulated enabled him to instruct those students who were reading below their grade using special materials which they could handle. He discovered students who knew nothing of structural and phonetic analysis. Furthermore, some students evidenced inability to read for the main idea and others had difficulty with inference skills. Thus, he was able to group his students for instruction not only on the basis of reading level but also on the basis of specific skill needs.

Various Factors Contributing to Failure to Learn to Read

The causes of failure to learn to read are always multiple, and although the classroom teacher is not a specialist in physical and emotional causes of reading failure, he needs to be conscious of the part these factors play in the reading performance of his students. He also needs to consider environmental, motivational or interest deficiencies which may exist. Spache wrote (*21*):

> In the fullest sense of the term, a reading diagnosis is intended to help us understand how the present reading performances are a projection of the reader's self-concept, how they reflect his physical and emotional adjustments to academic demands or to life in general. Reading behaviors are frequently an expression of the reader's attitudes toward the reading task. For example, he may read slowly because of anxiety, distaste for reading, lack of self-confidence, neurotic perfectionism, or rigidity. The emotional reactions to reading are the basic causes of poor rate as often as the more mechanical factors of habit, poor vocabulary, and lack of rate training. In addition to

these emotional causes, variations in visual, auditory and intellectual powers contribute to reading retardation. Simple description of the present reading skills ignores the role of all the major factors which may be contributing to the reading disability.

Since reading is a visual act, the teacher must always be conscious of the importance of visual acuity, visual functioning, and directional attack —the three components of vision. Too long have we used visual tests which only screen for near-sightedness or far-sightedness. This, then, is the teachers' first responsibility in the vision area: to have his students' vision tested by screening devices such as the Keystone Visual Survey Tests (11) and the Spache Binocular Reading Test (19). Many schools routinely screen pupils' vision every year or every two years with these devices or similar ones. As a result of giving the Visual Survey Tests, the tester knows thirteen things about the way in which this person sees, including vision functioning. A large number of students who read poorly do so because of fusion problems, vertical or lateral imbalance, or suppression of vision in one eye. Since schools do not provide visual specialists, teachers or nurses must assume responsibility to screen, identify, and refer visual problems to vision experts. As a classroom practitioner, the teacher can work faithfully on the improvement of reading skills, but if the student has a visual acuity or visual functioning problem, it will be of little avail. So fundamental to achievement in reading is the vision problem that it must have attention before much progress will result. (Read George Spache's *Toward Better Reading,* Chapter 6, "Diagnosis of Reading Disability.")

Some disability cases in reading have directional difficulties (i.e., a confusion of left-right shapes and movement) which is the third component of vision. Although no one has satisfactorily explained the *cause* of confusion in letters of similar shapes, such as *b* and *d,* or the reversal of the words *saw* and *was,* or the tendency of some readers to prefer to move from right to left in print instead of left to right, as the reading of English demands, all teachers have observed students with one or more of these problems. In order for proper remediation to be given, the classroom teacher needs to identify those students whom he has observed and refer them to a remedial reading specialist or clinician. Clearly the responsibility of the classroom teacher in this area is one of identification and referral to specialists who can determine the extent and nature of the difficulty, and provide remedial measures.

Auditory malfunctions occur less frequently than visual abnormalities.

But, because of the relation of listening to reading, teachers need to use informal methods of observation in order to screen their classes for auditory difficulties. Such behavior as tilting the head, continual inattention, watching the speaker's lips, etc., may be clues to loss of hearing. Bond and Tinker (3) suggest informal "watch ticking" and "whisper" tests.

A loud-ticking watch, such as an Ingersoll or a Westclox Pocket Ben is employed for the watch-tick test. The child with normal hearing will hear the usual ticking at a distance of about 48 inches. Testing is done in a quiet room. The child stands with one ear toward the examiner and puts his finger in the other ear. The examiner holds a card beside the child's head so that he cannot see the watch. Then the watch is held close to the child's ear and gradually withdrawn until it can no longer be heard. The distance at which the ticking is first heard is recorded. An average of the two distances is taken. If this average is less than 20 inches, the child requires further checking.

The following method has been used successfully by the writers for administering the whisper or low-voice test: Four or five children are lined up in a row in a quiet room about 5 feet from the examiner and with their backs to him. The latter remains in a fixed position and gives directions to the children, speaking in a distinct, low tone of voice. Directions such as the following are given: "Take five steps forward; raise your right arm; take two steps forward; hold up three fingers"; etc. By watching the children, the examiner can note those who hesitate, turn to see what other children do, look back at the examiner, or fail to follow directions. The children who get to a position approximately 20 feet from the examiner without signs of seeking help have normal hearing. Hard-of-hearing children are readily detected. Whisper tests may be given by softly saying single words while the child stands about 20 feet away with one ear turned toward the examiner. i.e., a distance at which the majority of children can hear in the particular room used. The child attempts to repeat each word as he hears it. If necessary, the examiner moves closer until responses are correct. Each ear is tested separately.

Again, the role of the teacher here is that of identifying students with such problems and referring them to an expert.

In some disability cases, severe illnesses may be a contributing factor. Items which might relate directly to the reading disability in the area of physical experiences are: severe childhood illnesses, head injuries, glandular malfunctions, unconsciousness for any duration of time, serious allergies, prolonged sinus infection, etc.

There are many psychological causes of failure in reading. Emotional problems may be so severe that the student is "blocked" in his efforts to learn. The extent of the severity and the source of the distress, of course, determines how much the factor will operate against normal progress. A mild emotional problem may be one which the student can overcome, if feelings of confidence and accomplishment are built into the reading situation. Many teachers have shown students how they can be independent in the area of word attack skills, for example, and have thereby helped to balance the emotional problem with success. At the other end of the scale, the student may be a seriously disturbed person and in need of professional help from a psychologist or psychiatrist.

Many emotional problems have their roots in the student's home and school environment. Although there are not many things a teacher can do to improve the home environment, he can recognize the problem and deal sympathetically with the student, adapting the techniques she uses with him to knowledge of the pupil's background. In so doing, the teacher creates a school climate favorable to success by producing a friendly, compassionate environment in his classroom. Perhaps, in many of our overcrowded urban high schools there is nothing needed so desperately today as this kind of classroom setting. Roswell and Natchez (16) express somewhat the same idea:

> In assessing emotional factors in children with reading disability, it has often been assumed that such children suffer from an emotional disturbance which must be cleared up through some form of psychotherapy before they can benefit optimally from reading instruction. This assumption is highly questionable not only because our theoretical framework is as yet on shaky foundations, but because a great number of children with reading disability may be displaying emotional disturbance as a direct reaction to their poor schoolwork. In addition, poor performance in school reinforces and intensifies any emotional disturbance that was already present.

Although some students may have no physical or emotional problems, many have educational reasons for not developing in reading. Consider the record of one student. He began the first grade with fifty-nine other six-year-olds. In the spring, he had the measles, mumps, and chickenpox which caused frequent absences. In second grade, he had a teacher who had no previous classroom experience but who had served as the clerk in the office. In the third grade his family moved three times. Being a shy boy, he failed to adjust to any of these changes, and by this time found himself far behind the average reader. In the fourth grade he had his first opportunity to make progress, but was enrolled in a school which made little effort to meet individual differences. Two more moves in successive years left this youngest at a second grade reading level when he enteerd junior high school. The *chief factor* responsible for this student's disability must be considered educational.

A host of other causes of reading difficulty might be listed as miscellaneous. The classroom teacher, even as the clinician, has little to guide him in the neurological area. Positive answers to certain problems remain unanswered. These problems are: brain damage, neurological complications, directional attack, letter confusions, aphasia, etc.

All teachers know that a lack of interest based upon the lack of a desire to learn to read or to improve in reading, is the basic problem of many who are behind in reading achievement. Discovering interests and motivating a desire to read has long been considered the hallmark of good teaching. Formal and informal ways have been devised to accomplish these ends. Most teachers find the informal ways more practical, although formal interest inventories are valuable, too, to reinforce and perhaps expand the information gained from conversations with students and in discussions of stories and content materials. Records often facilitate the teacher's use of knowledge gained in relation to student interests. Commercial devices, such as "My Reading Design" (*23*), often stimulate students to expand their range of interests.

Summary

In many ways diagnostic techniques for classroom use demand a new set of attitudes by the classroom teacher as he follows the trend of using informal devices, as well as formal ones, for obtaining pertinent information concerning his students. The results of standardized mental ability tests must be handled judiciously and techniques may include observation and listening as testing devices. While survey tests, diagnostic tests, and reading tests which accompany basal readers yield information on reading achievement, the informal reading inventory has proven its worth at all educational levels. The causes of some reading disabilities are easily discernible, although others elude not only classroom teachers but also the reading specialist. The multiple causes of reading retardation indicate the complexity of the reading process.

REFERENCES

1. Austin, Mary; Bush, Clifford; and Huebner, Mildred. *Reading Evaluation*. New York: The Ronald Press, 1961, 36.

2. Betts, Emmett A. *Foundations of Reading Instruction*. New York: American Book Co., 1957, 448.

3. Bond, Guy and Tinker, Miles A. *Reading Difficulties, Their Diagnosis and Correction*. New York: Appleton-Century-Crofts, Inc., 1957, 94-95.

4. *California Test of Mental Maturity* (California Test Bureau, 1957).

5. *Diagnostic Reading Tests*, Survey Section (Committee on Diagnostic Reading Tests, Inc., 1947-1952).

6. *Durrell-Sullivan Reading Capacity and Achievement Tests*, (World Book Co., 1945).

7. *Gates Reading Survey*, Bureau of Publications, Teachers College, Columbia University, 1958.

8. Harris, Albert J. *How to Increase Reading Ability*. New York: Longmans, Green and Company, 1956, 301.

9. *Iowa Silent Reading Tests* (World Book Co., 1927-1943).

10. Johnson, Marjorie Seddon and Kress, Roy A. *Informal Reading Inventories*. Newark, Delaware: International Reading Association, 1965.

11. *Keystone Visual Survey Tests* (Keystone View Company, 1954).

12. McDonald, Arthur. *Today's Challenges in the Teaching of Reading*, Proceedings of the Southern California Intermediate Council of the International Reading Association Conference, Beverly Hills, California, 1965.

13. Niles, Olive; Bracken, Dorothy Kendall; Dougherty, Mildred; and Kinder, Robert. *Tactics I and Tactics II*. Chicago: Scott, Foresman and Company, 1961 and 1964.

14. *Primary Mental Abilities Test* (Science Research Assoc., 1963).

15. Robinson, H. Alan. *The Underachiever in Reading*, Proceedings of the Annual Conference on Reading held at the University of Chicago. Chicago: The University of Chicago Press, 1962, 35.

16. Roswell, Florence and Natchez, Gladys. *Reading Disability, Diagnosis and Treatment*. New York: Basic Books, Inc., 1964, 55.

17. Smith, Nila Banton. *American Reading Instruction*. Newark, Delaware: International Reading Association, 1965, 302.

18. Smith, Nila Banton. *Graded Selections for Informal Reading Diagnosis, Grades Four Through Six*. New York: New York University Press, 1959.

19. *Spache Binocular Reading Test* (Keystone View Company).

20. Spache, George D. *Diagnostic Reading Scales*, Examiner's Manual, California Test Bureau, 1963, 5.

21. Spache, George D. *Toward Better Reading*. Champaign, Illinois: Garrard Publishing Company, 1963, 101-102.

22. Strang, Ruth and Bracken, Dorothy Kendall. *Making Better Readers*. Boston: D. C. Heath and Company, 1957, 73.

23. Strang, Ruth. *Diagnostic Teaching of Reading*. New York: McGraw-Hill Book Company, 1964, 52-55, 73.

NANCY O'NEILL VICK

JUNIOR HIGH SCHOOLS, FORT WORTH, TEXAS

4. The Role of a Reading Consultant in a Content Area Classroom

IN THE SECONDARY SCHOOL, approximately 85 percent of the learning which takes place is based on reading. Yet today we are retaining in school many students who, in former years, would have dropped out because of their inability to read adequately. Textbooks are becoming increasingly difficult in the content areas as new discoveries, new developments, and new concepts are added to or replace former information. Libraries, both central and classroom, enrich and supplement the curriculum, but increase the reading load of students. Small wonder that individuals who are already behind their classmates in reading ability often despair of meeting the increasing demands of their teachers.

Today, also, teachers must keep pace with the current knowledge explosion. They are having to learn and teach new discoveries, new developments, and new concepts. They, too, are faced with ever-expanding libraries which increase their reading load. Small wonder that some teachers despair of meeting the increasing demands of their pupils.

It is at this point that the reading consultant can be of service to both teachers and students. It is the reading consultant who can help teachers to recognize and to understand students with reading problems. It is the consultant who can assist teachers in applying the special study skills needed in each subject, and who can suggest special study methods. Also, the reading consultant can demonstrate ways to teach vocabulary effectively and methods of increasing comprehension. Finally, the reading consultant can help the teachers with both the selection and use of multi-level books and materials so that teachers can more nearly meet the individual needs of their students.

Know Your Pupils

What must consultants do first in order to improve the reading skills in content classes? They must help teachers to meet their students on the corners where the students stand! One does not lead a person whose hand he misses by a city block, nor does one teach a student whose instructional level he misses by several grade levels. Contact must be made—and maintained—between the teacher and the students. The reading consultant can help the teachers to locate these individuals, and to make provision to meet them "on their own ground."

The first indication of the corners on which the students stand may be gained by checking their reading levels. This will provide the teacher with the instructional level of each individual. It is at this level of difficulty that students can read *with proper* instruction. Any independent reading required of them should be one or two levels below this level. The reading consultant can assist the content area teacher in locating materials which are appropriate for their students' levels of ability. A student who is approximately fourth grade reading level can not be reached via a ninth grade level book.

Next, the teacher must be cognizant of the general characteristics of students who are in need of corrective reading. Knowing these, he can then plan work suitable for his students (7). However, there is no substitute for a teacher who is sensitive to individual differences, for that which motivates one individual may embarrass or antagonize another. For that reason, the teacher must make a continuous effort to discern the reactions of each individual, then plan future strategy accordingly.

Another consideration which influences both teaching methods and materials is the individual's mental ability, for this affects both his learning capacity and his rate of learning. In general, the less intelligent child will have greater difficulty with reading. He frequently lacks curiosity, a quality basic to learning. Often, too, he lacks the ability to reason, to see cause-and-effect relationships, and to generalize. The consultant can help teachers understand these characteristics which are typical of the slow learner.

However, teachers must be cautious in applying the slow-learner label to individuals (4). Bright students who cannot read adequately will score low on an intelligence test based on reading. Adverse home environment, bad health, and poor teaching can produce these same symptoms in average or even bright students. One needs always to remember that Edison, Newton, and Einstein were thought to have been slow learners!

The students in need of corrective reading are usually lacking in fluency and precision of speech. Their vocabularies are frequently meager and inadequate. While their own speech is usually replete with colorful metaphors, they fail to comprehend figurative expressions in written language. The consultant can help the teacher develop many activities which involve spoken language to help overcome this problem.

Furthermore, the attention span of low achievers is frequently quite limited. They are easily distracted, or drift off into day dreams which completely "tune out" the teacher and the class. Yet when one observes the same students working painstakingly for long periods of time on their hot-rods or their aquariums, one realizes that there is a relationship between attention on the one hand and interest and motivation on the other. The consultant can help the teacher to make the work more interesting and to diversify the activities wisely. Together they can plan ways to motivate the students to want to learn.

Most students who are having difficulty read virtually everything at the same speed. The consultant can help the teacher to identify the various rates of reading so that each individual may be taught to adjust his rates to the material he is reading, and to his purpose for reading.

The slower the student, the more immediate are his goals and aspirations. Bright students, and frequently average students, develop long-range goals: they plan for tomorrow. But for these slower readers, today is the total of time. Yesterday has been enshrouded in an almost impenetrable shell of indifference and frustration. Tomorrow may never come. Only what happens today is important. Therefore, the teacher must make the material which is being presented necessary for today; it must be immediately practical. When immediate needs can be met successfully, the slower students become quite as excited about their achievements as the brighter students do. On the other hand, they are much more easily discouraged and disheartened, and require the constant bolstering of the teacher in order to maintain a consistent work pattern. The reading consultant can help the classroom teacher to understand these fundamental personality differences. He can also assist the teacher in planning so that each lesson will involve some practical application of the concept being studied.

"Schools have been giving their students tools in the expectation that the students themselves will work out the necessary techniques for using them. As often happens, the gifted and the experienced can work with the crudest instruments, whereas the novice and the slow-learner remain helpless with the best" (*3*). The slow learners also need to know how to use that which they are learning. They are unable to make this transfer unaided by the teacher.

Study Skills

The reading consultant can assist all teachers in outlining the study skills necessary for effective learning (*1*). Yes, teachers do know how to study, yet many of them have developed these skills to such a high degree that they are carried out almost unconsciously. Consequently, the teacher may have some difficulty in defining and separating the various study skills so that they can be taught effectively.

Direct teaching of the study skills will help every student, the college-bound or the terminal. Even though many of these skills are common to all learning, the very immaturity of the students in our schools makes it inadvisable to risk anything as fundamental as leaving the study skills to chance. The teacher in each subject must teach students how to apply the specific skills needed in his own subject. The bright will see the relationships quickly and can proceed to apply them immediately. The slower will need repeated assistance in applying the various skills until at last they become habitual.

Perhaps the first duty of the teachers is to teach the skills of locating information. The most obvious—and therefore the most neglected one—is the use of the various parts of the textbook. Practice in using the table of contents, the glossary, the preface, the index, and the title page will benefit all students. Exercises for teaching these can be devised easily. They will also provide an excellent way of introducing the textbook to the class and of presenting an overview of the course. Such exercises are effective because the students have a part—an active part—in each step of the presentation. By using an overhead projector, the teacher can be sure that students are following instructions and are able to take part in the class discussion and, later, in the drills and application.

A transparency made of each page to be presented will permit the teacher to mask all the material but the specific item to which he is referring. Students can locate this in their own textbook, then discuss the importance of the item. After each important part has been presented and discussed, the teacher may have a contest to see who can locate information fastest by using the various parts of the book.

An open book quiz or an exercise for homework might include the following questions:

1. When was this book published?
2. Why is this date important?
3. Where is the index?
4. What does the index contain?
5. How is the index organized?
6. Where is the table of contents located?
7. How is the table of contents organized?
8. Where is the glossary?
9. What is the glossary?
10. What is the preface?
11. Read the preface of this book, and tell, in your own words, why the author wrote the preface. Be brief.
12. Who wrote the book? Do you think he is qualified to write such a book? Why?

Chapter titles, headings, review questions, and summaries are excellent study aids. The teacher may use these in many ways. One effective use is to teach students how to set up their own purposes for reading. The teacher may have students read only the chapter title and the section headings. Then, he may have one individual read aloud the review questions. Others may close their books and develop a list of questions which they think this chapter will answer. The teacher will list these questions on the chalkboard. Then the students may reopen their books and examine pictures, charts, or graphs. Again, they should close books and check questions which are on the chalkboard and revise them, deleting any which now seem unimportant, adding those which now appear to be important. Teacher and learners may now discuss which parts of the chapter must be read very slowly and carefully and which may be skimmed. Now, the teacher may have the chapter read silently having students adjust their rate of reading to the purpose for which they are reading. This technique of surveying the chapter will be particularly useful all through the year as an important study technique.

Most content area textbooks are expository and lend themselves well to the teaching of outlining, another basic study skill. Outlining is difficult for many students to master, but the consultant can suggest ways to help. One effective way is to have students fill in the details of an outline for which they have been given the main ideas. Then they may compare their outlines with a teacher-made one. This is an exercise which also is well-suited to the overhead projector. The main ideas may be written on the static transparency, then an overlay prepared with the details. Or, the students can fill in the details on the transparency with a grease pencil. This will involve more of them in the outlining process and will make it more meaningful.

Expository material lends itself well to the teaching of note-taking. Too many learners, especially those who have problems with reading, instead of making notes, copy the material verbatim from an encyclopedia or a reference book, and understand nothing. This copying should be discouraged except when an exact quotation is desired. Students should be taught first to read for key sentences, then to be aware of supporting details. They must also learn to watch for transitional words which serve as road signs indicating what is to follow. It will take many instances of developing notes as a class exercise before students can "be on their own" in note-taking. Exercises such as the one which follows will hasten the day of independence and may be devised easily.

1. Make a series of transparencies, each containing one good paragraph. Use some paragraphs with the key sentence coming as the first sentence. Use some with a summary sentence. Use some with an imbedded key sentence, and a few with the key idea not explicitly stated. Put a transparency on the overhead projector. Have students read it silently, and copy the sentence they think is the key sentence. Have various individuals each read the sentence he selected as the key sentence and justify his selection. Now mark on the transparency the correct sentence. Be sure they all understand why it is correct. Begin with the easiest transparency, the key sentence first in the paragraph, and progress slowly to the most difficult transparency, the one with the implied key idea.

2. Teach students to watch for such statements as the following: "Three major terms of the treaty," "Several uses of peroxide are," "In the first place," "next," "finally." These usually carry the supporting details.

3. Words like "but," "yet," "however," "on the contrary," are warning signs that a contradictory statement is coming. Have them watch for these. "And," "moreover," "also," which indicate additional facts.

It is often necessary to teach slower students how to use the notes which they have taken or the outline they have developed. The first day, the teacher may have them read the expository material; then, with them, work out the notes or the outline, whichever is being taught. The following day, the teacher may have the students place their notes in front of them.

One may read an item aloud; then all may discuss it. In the beginning stages, this will take much prompting and encouragement by the teacher. After several practice sessions, students will begin to utilize the techniques of taking notes on their own.

The reading of maps, graphs, and charts takes direct teaching also. Many times, if students can produce a bar graph, a line graph, a pictorial graph, a map, or a chart, they will have a better understanding of these graphic representations as they see them in a text. A circle graph showing the percentage of students in each grade in their school can be a beginning assignment. A map of the campus with the appropriate legends on it may be made. Then the teacher may progress to other exercises involving the reading of commercial maps. He may use city maps and have students locate their homes. State maps will allow students to plan an imaginary weekend excursion, giving the directions, highways, and distances from the road map. The reading consultant can frequently provide materials for these exercises.

Time should be spent at the beginning of the year in presenting to students a good method of study (2). Research shows that one reading of text materials, done properly, is as valuable as several readings done in a purposeless, haphazard way. Several methods are current, with most of them following a similar pattern of first setting a purpose for the reading; then, the actual reading; and finally, some kind of review to clinch learnings. In this age of advertising slogans and competition for student time, the method should have a "catchy" title and an easily remembered formula.

The Survey Q3R Method (5) is a widely-used study technique recommended by many reading consultants. Devised by Francis P. Robinson, it is commonly taught under its original name—Survey Q3R —or in various adaptations. It generally involves the following steps:*

1. *Survey* the material by reading headings, topic and summary sentences and, perhaps, the introductory and summary paragraphs.
2. *Question*—Questions to guide the careful reading are structured by the teacher, or by the student as a result of the surveying. Questions may also be formulated from the headings or main ideas. Thus the reading is planned in terms of specific purposes, such as answering the questions or recognizing the organization. At this time, the student also makes tentative plans in terms of the speed and degree of attention to detail

---

*This summary is taken from *Toward Better Reading* by George Spache, Garrard Publishing Company, Champaign, Illinois, 1963, p. 345.

with which he will read.

3. *Read*—The material is now read thoroughly and carefully in a manner intended to accomplish the purposes outlined previously.

4. *Recite*—A self-recitation is undertaken to determine the pupil's ability to recall the content of the material and to answer the questions he has proposed to himself.

5. *Review*—As a result of the self-recitation, the student knows which sections of the material he should review for more thorough understanding or recall.

Vocabulary

Students who are deficient in reading skills often lack an adequate vocabulary. Words are the building blocks—or, for some students, the stumbling blocks—of reading. Each subject matter teacher must assume the responsibility for teaching the specialized vocabulary of his subject. Here, again, the reading consultant can be helpful in suggesting ways in which words may be introduced, in suggesting which words may give the students some difficulty, and in keeping the teachers informed about the standardized test results which have to do with vocabulary.

Linguists teach us that words are symbols of reality. We know that reading is the association of a given symbol with a word. In short, the printed word is the symbol of a symbol. Small wonder, then, that the young person who finds abstractions to be difficult, also finds that reading is a tiring task that demands more from him than he is willing to give. The consultant may help the teacher in presenting new words to students in such a manner that the gap from symbol to reality may be more easily bridged.

1. Realia should be used whenever it is possible. "Pretend" jewels, purchased at the variety store, can be viewed, handled, and compared, thus making the words topaz, emerald, pearl, amethyst more of a reality. Students should use these words orally, then in written sentences. After this, a bulletin board display with a small treasure chest with these "jewels" spilling out of it will serve as a daily reminder (with teacher prompting) of the new words. Following this teaching, these words in print will have meaning. Similarly, a piece of velvet, a piece of sandpaper, a piece of alabaster may give the student first-hand experience with a word.

2. When the new word is a verb, frequently the teacher can dramatize it. Such words as trudge, dissent, drawl, scowl can be demonstrated. Science, homemaking, and industrial arts teachers are indeed

fortunate, for by the very nature of their subject matter, they can demonstrate many words.

3. When first-hand experience with the word is impossible, then the use of vicarious experience is indicated. Pictures on the bulletin board, films, filmstrips, pictures in books, or transparencies used on the overhead projector frequently make good substitutes for reality.

All of us remember with fond delight the kindergarten child who excitedly announced to her mother at the end of her first school day, "Teacher says you have to buy me a gun for school tomorrow."

The mother, disbelieving the strange demand, countered with, "Tell me the exact words your teacher said, dear."

"She said, 'When you come back tomorrow, I'm going to teach you how to draw,' and she can't teach me unless I have a gun!" exclaimed the young Annie Oakley.

Words have many meanings: to dress a doll and to dress a chicken; to baste a skirt and to baste the roast; to set the table, to table the motion, the multiplication table, the table of contents, the tableland, to turn the tables—these are but a few of the words in English which have multiple meanings. In fact, multiple-meanings of words are so common and we adults use them so frequently that it is sometimes difficult to remember that everyone may not know the correct meaning unless the context is clear. The content area teacher must remember to teach the meaning that is correct for that subject.

Idiomatic expressions cause much difficulty, particularly to bilingual students. "Treading on thin ice," "to pay the piper," "to face the music," "to be called on the carpet," "to roll out the red carpet" are but a few. When such an expression comes up in class, the teacher may explain it as best he can. Then, have students write a short paragraph in which the expression is used in the key sentence. Have the best of these read aloud to the class. Youngsters do speak the same language, and can frequently explain to each other such expressions in a more understandable way than most adults can.

Although the English teacher usually assumes the responsibility for teaching the structure of words, each teacher will find that some structural analysis of new vocabulary will help students to understand and to remember the new words more easily. For example, the science teacher who teaches first the Greek roots, *geo* and *bio,* relating them to known words of geography and biography, will find students understanding more easily the new science terms. Teaching the root *ptero* can assist in both the spelling of new scientific terms and the understanding of such classifications. The root word *meter* means *measure* in words used in science or mathematics, and makes such words as *hydrometer, thermometer* and *millimeter* more meaningful. Mathematics, science, social studies, and English can all benefit from studying prefixes derived from foreign numerals. Think of the word meanings which become understandable when we know that *ambi, bin, bi, bis, duo, di,* and *twi* all carry the meaning of *two!* The other numerals from one to ten also are represented by various prefixes which are helpful because they will unlock the meanings of many new words.

Some knowledge of suffixes is also valuable. Science students will find *-ous, -ic,* and other suffixes to be particularly helpful. Other much-used suffixes, *-able, -ible, -ful, -er, -or, -ment, -ward, -ive,* if the meanings are known, can extend the pupil's vocabulary rapidly.

The consultant may need to assist teachers to understand that research shows that words, taught in context, tend to be remembered better than words taught in isolation. Also, teachers will want to be reminded of the value of frequent reviews of words new to students.

One cannot leave the discussion of word study and the development of meanings without mention of the dictionary. While over-dependence on this tool is not desirable, efficient and intelligent use of the dictionary is necessary for good scholarship. All teachers should teach students to use the guide words and the key words. Each teacher should call attention to the source of the word, and, perhaps, to other forms of the word. The number of possible definitions should be noted; then, students should be taught to find the definition that fits into the context of the material. Students are likely to take the first definition the dictionary lists, whether or not it "makes sense" in the sentence. Teachers need to develop in the students the habit of demanding meaning from the sentences which they read. This is sometimes difficult to do when the reader has for years formed the habit of reading words but not demanding any meaning from them.

Teachers can help learners to gain a better concept of the meaning of a word by calling attention to the illustrations which are in the dictionary. However, the slow student is frequently not aware of the significance of the little fraction beside the picture of the note "three feet high at shoulder" which appears beneath the illustration. If this is explained, or if the size is drawn to exact measurements on the chalkboard, he will have a better understanding of the meaning or the word. If this is not done, some student will decide that a minnow and a whale are the same size since the illustrations are the same size!

Because nothing succeeds like success, all teachers should encourage students to keep a vocabulary list of new words which they have learned. These words should be reviewed frequently enough that they will really become a part of the students' speaking, reading, and writing vocabularies. Such lists, *when students really know the meanings of the words,* provide a genuine sense of accomplishment and satisfaction.

Increasing Comprehension

It is hardly reasonable to expect every teacher to be an expert teacher of reading (8). It is reasonable to expect every teacher to know some of the aspects of the teaching of reading which will improve comprehension in his subject. These aspects the reading consultant can demonstrate by teaching a class for the subject-teacher. While no consultant will usurp the classroom teacher's position, teachers should feel free to ask the consultant to come in and teach a lesson for them to observe. This benefits the consultant by affording continuing classroom experiences for him; it benefits the teacher by permitting him to view his class objectively while he watches another person at work with his students. Also, the classroom teacher can see how another person adapts the general principles of the teaching of reading to a specific subject and a specific class.

The following activities which will help to increase the students' comprehension skills can easily be demonstrated by the consultant and can be adapted by the teacher to other lessons.

First, words new to students must be anticipated and taught. It is no more reasonable to expect them to read English words which are completely unknown to them than it is to expect them to read foreign words. This topic has been previously discussed, and is mentioned here only as a reminder that this is a basic first step in the reading approach to any learning.

Next, meaning developed from phrases and sentences is more than the sum of the meanings of the individual words. "Cold-hearted" is not a statement of the heart's physical temperature, but of a personality characteristic. "Hot-headed," "sharp-tongued," "soft drink," "top brass" all carry specialized phrase meanings. "In the water" and "on the water" are phrases which differ by only one letter, but the difference in meaning of the sentences "He walked in the water" and "He walked on the water" is staggering. Teachers must be sure that students understand phrases, that they group the right words together into phrases, and that the words in the phrases are correctly read.

The next logical step in reading is for the student to understand sentences. Students should be able to pick out the subject and the verb in most sentences. This will help them to identify what is being talked about and what happened. If they are so deficient in language skills that this is difficult for them to do, the "telegram" technique often works. This requires them to reduce the sentence to its bare essentials—the subject and the verb and perhaps the complement—without having to consider the grammatical terms which, to some, form a block. However, other students can readily apply this use of the study of grammar to reading if teachers will only point out the connection to them.

In both long sentences and in paragraphs, the "reporter" method of analyzing the selection will assist many in identifying the salient points. In this exercise, the teacher will list in a column the five W's and H which journalists use in reporting, leaving a blank space after each for the student to fill in. The exercise would read thus:

Read the assigned paragraph. Then answer the questions in the blanks provided. Be brief.

Who?
What?
Where?
When?
Why?
How?

Teachers can introduce this exercise by using an overhead projector and working out the first answers with the class.

In addition to the teaching of outlining and note-taking, which have already been discussed, teachers will find that having students write short summaries in their own words forces them to read for meaning. Since this demands reorganization of the author's materials, it is a difficult and comparatively high-level reading skill.

Teachers of industrial arts, science, art, and other laboratory classes are particular fortunate in having materials with which they can give concrete examples of their subject matter. Teachers should take full advantage of this opportunity. However, social studies and English are not so happily situated. Consequently, the teachers of these subjects need to take advantage of the available films, filmstrips, and the overhead projector with its inexhaustible—depending upon the teacher's alertness and certainty—supply of transparencies. They also need to use records, tape recorders, and any other available audio-visual aids in order to recreate the past or to make the distant and the foreign near-at-hand and understandable. Field trips, whenever they are possible, are needed to build a background of experience for many young people. However, when it is impossible to take them to the far away places, these must be brought to class via modern audio-visual aids.

Behind-the-Scenes Duties

Just as the activities which are pertinent to teaching include many things other than the actual minutes spent before the class, so the activities which are pertinent to the work of a reading consultant in relationship to the content classroom involve many activities other than the demonstration class. Before and after class, the teacher performs those tasks which make teaching a success or doom it to failure. Lesson planning, arranging the classroom and assembling the equipment, grading and studying papers, the reading, studying, and thinking which the teacher does away from the class are crucial to the act of teaching. Before and after the classroom visit and demonstration the consultant prepares to make his work of value to the teacher and to the students (6).

Students in need of help cannot be identified and their problems diagnosed unless the right tests are selected, properly administered, and the results correctly interpreted. All of this information must then be translated into good, classroom planning. The reading consultant needs to devote much time to the planning and the implementation of a good formal testing program.

The reading consultant must be expert in the use of informal evaluations as well as formal. No day should elapse without informal evaluation by the teacher, and the reading consultant can assist teachers in planning for these daily evaluations. Teacher-made tests, which are an important part of teaching and evaluation, should be familiar to the consultant so that help can be given to teachers in this crucial area. Guides can be developed to assist teachers, and the development of such bulletins, if prepared by teacher committees, will serve as excellent in-service training.

The reading consultant should be able to help teachers in developing the organization in their classrooms which will best implement the teaching that is needed. If test results show that students have a range of many years in their reading abilities, it is unrealistic to organize the class so that all will theoretically move together throughout the course. Teachers will need suggestions and demonstrations on when and how to group and on the use of multi-level materials that meet specific needs. Consultants need to be skillful in helping teachers develop the patterns of classroom grouping which will be most efficacious.

A rule-of-thumb guide to indicate the range of reading levels in the average classroom is two-thirds of the age of the students. This means that the average class of fifteen-year-old students will have a ten year span from the poorest reader to the best. For this reason a graded list of available books must be accessible to teachers and to librarians. This will need to be revised as new high-interest, low-reading-level materials come on the market. But such lists are valueless unless teachers are skillful in individualizing work. Just as one improves his swimming by practicing, one learns reading by reading. Again, the consultant should be able to help the teacher in this planning, both in the selection of books and in the effective use of them, to encourage wide reading by all.

Finally, research should always be a part of the program. As new equipment, new methods, and new books become available, they will need to be classroom tested to see whether or not they will aid the instructional program. But just because an item is new does not earn it a right to a classroom test. The consultant should read, check, observe, and consult others about such innovations. Those which look as though they have promise of strengthening the reading program should be classroom tested. This will involve the aid of classroom teachers, providing them with in-service training, and designing the proper evaluation so that the innovation will have a fair trial.

REFERENCES

1. Bamman, Henry A.; Hogan, Ursula; and Greene, Charles E. *Reading Instruction in Secondary Schools.*
2. Dechant, Emerald V. *Improving the Teaching of Reading.* Englewood Cliffs, N. J.: Prentice-Hall, 1964, 322-402.
3. Commission on English, *Freedom and Discipline in English.* Princeton, New Jersey: College Entrance Examination Board, 1965, 35.
4. Jewett, Arno; Mersand, Joseph; and Gunderson, Doris V. *Improving English Skills of Culturally Different Youth in Large Cities.* Washington, D. C.: U. S. Department of Health, Education and Welfare, 1964, 35-57.
5. Robinson, Francis P. *Effective Study,* Revised Edition. New York: Harper, Row and World, 1961, 13-48.
6. Robinson, H. Alan; and Rauch, Sidney, J. *Guiding the Reading Program.* Chicago: Science Research Associates, 1965, 25-38.
7. Strang, Ruth. *Diagnostic Teaching of Reading.* New York: McGraw-Hill Company, 1964, 27-58.
8. Strang, Ruth and Bracken, Dorothy. *Making Better Readers.* Boston: D. C. Heath and Company, 1957, 203-288.

LEITHA PAULSEN

AND

NANCY LARMER

BLOOM TOWNSHIP HIGH SCHOOL, CHICAGO HEIGHTS, ILLINOIS

5.Using Writing to Help the Poor Reader

TEACHERS have long assumed that a relationship between reading and writing exists and have long urged the union of composition and literature in the classroom. However, most of the attempts at integration have been futile, for they turn to reading assignments for nothing more than theme topics. The ways in which each dimension can be used to strengthen the other remain relatively unexplored.

When our school became involved in the task of writing a curriculum guide in composition, it became obvious that it would be necessary not only to examine the process of composing itself but also to investigate its relationship to literature. The results of our efforts to design a new curriculum suggest ways that reading and writing can be brought closer together so that one will facilitate learning the other.

We have given some thought to the notion that we can get the greatest returns from both writing and reading instruction if the emphasis is on writing first. Why begin with writing? It may well be through the painful process of organizing and composing that the student can grasp the full structure and meaning of what someone else has written. There is more psychological push to initiating a communication than there is to receiving one. Because writing is an intensive learning situation, the student learns better and retains longer. Skills which have become fixed through writing are more readily available for transfer to reading.

In considering the writing-to-reading emphasis, we have identified a number of concepts common to both the reading and writing processes. This paper discusses specific techniques related to two of these concepts: (1) the concept of structure, including both unity and coherence, and (2) the concept of specificity.

51

The Concept of Structure

Whether it deals with fact or fancy, whether it is an expository essay marshalling hard, cold facts or an emotion-stirring poem that meditates death, whether it is as short as a sentence or as long as a novel, all good writing has structure. It is never just an amorphous mass of words; instead, it is a pattern of words carefully shaped and fitted together in such a way as to create a harmonious whole. Many poor readers—and writers, too—see only the amorphous mass. They do not think in terms of examining the separate chunks or parts and then of the need to unify these chunks to arrive at the intended meaning. Even if the reader makes some such attempt, he often puts the pieces together in a random order without understanding that they must be disciplined in the same way that the writer himself disciplined them. Or he will disregard the multiplicity of parts and attach too much importance to just *one* of them, not understanding that the real meaning is the sum of *all* the parts. Obviously, none of these attempts establishes any real communication, for the communication itself has not been perceived as a structure. Structure, then, shapes meaning. And if structure—the parts of the whole and the relationships of these parts—shapes meaning, then students must be sensitive to structure in units of various sizes as well as forms of various kinds. The relationships among words in sentences, sentences in paragraphs, paragraphs in longer essays; the relationships of stanzas in poetry and elements in a short story—all should be taught at increasing levels of difficulty.

Recognizing the cruciality of this concept, teachers in our school have been devising and experimenting with writing-to-reading techniques that might lead students to recognition of structural unity. Two of these are known as the key word technique and the cognitive map technique.

With the key word technique, students are taught to strip sentences down to their essential message-carrying words so that the main idea-detail pattern in paragraphs stands out. The use of this idea, developed by Robinson (2), has been previously reported by others (1). It has, however, always been discussed as a technique for helping students recognize structure in their *reading*. We would like to suggest that we change the emphasis. Instead of using it as a device for merely pointing out structure in their reading, why not actively involve students and have them use it as a device for building structure into their writing? Surely if students become intimately concerned with the technique through the process of writing, there is greater likelihood that it will be used for problem-solving in reading.

The first step, then, is the unguided writing of a paragraph. Next, the class may be asked to look at a challenging paragraph sample. This should be viewed as writing, not reading—somebody wrote this; now what was he trying to say? Each student decides on a main idea and writes it down. The teacher polls the class members and writes on the board whatever variety of main ideas is suggested. The lack of agreement becomes obvious and along with this the need for a skill to help students decide what the writer is really saying is neatly established. Now, the key word technique is introduced. At this point, comparing to a telegram or cablegram helps to explain the principle; placing a dollar value on words keeps interest high. Students practice the technique together, reducing sentences placed on the board to their message-carrying elements.

Following work on single sentences, students transfer the key word skill to practice paragraphs. They list the key words from each sentence in a column, then note that all but one are details of the same density or value. This is the general statement that sums up the idea of all the others and is therefore the main idea. The class returns to the original sample, using the newly-learned technique to reach agreement on the correct answer.

Students now examine additional writing samples in order to establish two criteria for a well-structured paragraph: (1) that there be a clear statement of a topic idea; and (2) that it include only details which directly support that idea.

A topic sentence is often problematical. It must not only name the topic but also tell something about it. It is the lead sentence and as such whatever follows in the paragraph is directed by it. Therefore, it must sufficiently limit the subject and set up the goals to be achieved. The class first writes several topic sentences together; then they study paragraphs from which the topic sentences have been removed and write topic sentences of their own. This forces careful attention to each of the parts, for the topic sentence must cover everything; yet it cannot promise more than the sum of its parts will add up to.

Student paragraphs are returned and examined in groups in terms of the two criteria established. The students discover that their own paragraphs fall far short of achieving unity, but they now have some basis for revision. And in the process of revision itself the concept of structure is reinforced.

Once the students have this concept well in mind, we take them to selected paragraphs in their textbooks and ask them to impose the structure they have practiced to what someone else has written. In other words, we ask them to read for the main idea-related details pattern. So far, of course, we have achieved a good measure of success in bringing students to this point. Systematic use of the key word technique nearly always brings this result. What we are striving for, then, is that step beyond in which the student can not only apply the technique on demand, but does apply it as a matter of course on his own. Again, our idea is that the internalization of the concept of structure is more likely to occur through the writing process. We therefore move back to a writing activity, this time concentrating on making paragraphs better by adding a sufficient number of "juicy" details. Students are led again through the writing-evaluating-revising cycle, with the demand for "juiciness" contributing to the concept of completeness as an aspect of unity.

Now we turn back to reading—to apply what we know about the writing process there. The teacher leads students through a longer sample article, noting with them the key words of sentences; the main ideas of paragraphs; the details which support the main idea, calling special attention to the fact that supporting details for a single main idea may continue for several paragraphs. Following this detailed analysis, students are given a longer article to analyze and summarize on their own. They should at this point be able to attack the article intelligently and come up with a restatement of the author's main ideas. Hopefully, they will also habitually use the skill they have learned. While it is too early for us to offer any empirical evidence that this really does occur, we have a good deal of subjective evidence from the teachers who have used the technique. They report that students not only plan their own writing but they can see a plan in other's writing as well. And they remember better. Words are no longer just an amorphous mass to students for they can pick out main ideas and hang sub-details onto them.

It should be noted that writing and reading practice with the key word technique includes main ideas in a variety of positions within the paragraph: beginning, middle, end, within two or three sentences, and in a combination of first and last sentences. In addition to this comprehensive work with main ideas expressed, practice includes work with main ideas implied.

We do not claim that the technique is exciting. However, the description of the technique as given here is skeletal. Good teachers will bring to this framework activities and materials that will reflect the force of their own personalities. Nor do we claim that the technique is new. We feel, however, that our writing-to-reading emphasis adds a dimension which is worth consideration.

Another technique for dealing with the concept of unity in exposition has resulted from experimentation with programed learning directed by John Ginther at the University of Chicago. It involves carefully programed lessons in which teacher and student develop cognitive maps patterned after samples of good paragraph writing. Students follow a cognitive map in writing paragraphs of their own. The map prescribes the route that must be followed to accomplish the lesson's purpose—in this case, paragraph unity. It shows students where to begin and where they want to go and prescribes each step to be taken between the starting point and the destination.

Like the architect's plan the builder uses to erect a house, this is a precise plan to be followed in building paragraphs. A typical map for a paragraph containing a clear main idea statement fully developed by details would begin with a pattern for creating a main idea sentence. Thus, the student might be directed to name a person he knows, a group of people, or a familiar object. To this he would add "is always," or "is usually," or "always looks," and then conclude the sentence by naming a way his subject acts or looks. Following this pattern, a student might write a sentence like, "My little brother is always pretending." Having developed a main idea sentence, he is then directed to follow a very specific set of instructions, such as: (1) make a list of three or more details that could make your statement about your subject vividly clear to a reader; (2) for each detail you listed, write two good sentences, one of which introduces the detail and states it in a general way and one of which explains and clarifies your detail; (3) after the last detail sentence, write a sentence that makes some general statement about the subject of your paragraph, a statement that is based on the evidence you have presented. By following such a plan, even the slowest of students is more likely to build fully-developed and unified paragraphs.

Through a number of programed lessons, students examine samples of both good and bad writing, so that over a period of time, they develop several cognitive maps. The decisions they make in creating their maps are dictated by those things the teachers involved have decided are basic to composition: (1) unity—topic sentences that limit the subject and set up goals and are developed by pertinent details; (2) order—details that are not simply random but are carefully arranged for effect and for communicating true relationships; and (3) purpose—subjects that are treated subjectively or objectively depending on the particular message to be communicated, the writer's own attitude toward his message, and the audience toward which it is to be directed.

The similarity of these writing goals to those considered basic to reading is striking! In fact, the ideas dealt with and the student behavior demanded by both the key word and the cognitive map techniques are practically identical. Yet one was conceived as a writing-to-reading program while the other was conceived as a writing program only. We should note here that two groups of people worked independently to structure programs—one to aid reading, the other to aid writing—yet came up with the same behaviors to be developed. We have some subjective evidence that the writing-to-reading program works. Therefore, asking students to do the same thing, regardless of purpose, should also produce results. What this confirms, of course, is that reading and writing are highly interrelated by organization. An awareness of what goes into his own *writing* must surely increase a student's awareness of what he should draw out of his *reading!*

We recognize that teachers have long used some sort of outlining technique in teaching both writing and reading. Our use of these techniques is different only in the conception of the individual lesson as a highly structured, step-by-step process, which moves through a pre-determined sequence. Both techniques were developed in this way because of two basic assumptions: that students learn best if they know what steps they need to take to solve a problem, and that there is a greater likelihood that they will meet with success if the separate steps are small and lead to attainable goals. But what about this emphasis on structure? Are we trying to reduce creativity to a formula? By forcing students into methods of development, by giving them maps to follow, are we stifling the unconscious creativity that might otherwise emerge? Of course there will always be the successful unschooled papers. The unschooled paper, however, is like the work of the primitive artist. Teach a primitive artist and he may lose his art. So it is with the writer. The freshness and reality of his unschooled attempts may be lost when we put him into a harness. His unharnessed flair, however, will not serve him in demanding situations. Because his needs in composition become steadily more sophisticated and rigorous, we must attempt to school his "primitive" writing.

Whitehead's conception of education as movement from freedom to discipline and back to freedom again has application here (3). When we try to move a student from freedom to discipline, we must expect an attendant loss of spontaneity. His writing may lack its previous freshness and honesty but it will gain in structure. And, once he gets used to working within this structure, he can then reach out for new powers of expression, more potent now because they are marshalled by a basic framework.

This delineates for us the three kinds of writing behavior we can expect of our students. Some few of our students can never be disciplined. They will retain their primitive art and will occasionally, by some accident of circumstance, succeed. Many of our students will accept the discipline willingly, and find it safe and comfortable. Although they will never go beyond it, they will find in the discipline itself that they can indeed produce something, where nothing before existed. Other students, although they chafe at discipline for a while, will learn to use it as a tool. And with this tool, they will be able to achieve even more than was previously possible.

Beyond unity, another aspect of structure to be considered is coherence. To ignore the structural devices which change meaning is to get a distorted message. Of course, teachers have always pointed out devices of coherence. But mere "show and tell" has apparently helped little; for, in spite of training, students still do not use these devices or signals well. Perhaps we can establish the use of these signals in reading by demanding their use in writing.

Word order itself is an important signal to meaning. If the student is to deal with much of the literature in our books and anthologies, then he must understand not only the basic subject-verb-object structure of language, but beyond this he must see that a writer uses many deviations from this normal structure and creates from it many complex formations.

One way to help students become aware of the variety and complexity of structure is to have them build sentences of their own. Starting with a simple subject-verb-object skeleton, students can be taught to stretch the sentence by adding adjective or adverb modifiers, appositives, participial or prepositional phrases, and clauses. Thus, ways to build more mature sentence patterns can be explored. Also, students can learn to manipulate these patterns, changing order of placement and therefore relationships and meaning as well. They can learn, for example, that a shift in the placement of a subordinate conjunction can make the same sentence tell a different story. "When Mother turned her head, the baby drank her coffee," can be turned into "Mother turned her head when the baby drank her coffee." Both are correct, but the meaning has certainly changed!

After this specific practice on sentence variety and complexity, students can be directed to analyze their own compositions. In this analysis, they will most likely discover frequent use of a simple and compound sentence pattern. They should now be able to judge which of these sentences are effective as they stand; those that are immature and ineffective they should be able to revise in such a way that they better signal the meaning intended.*

Students can be alerted to word order not only by generating sentences of their own but also by imitating models. In imitation, our concern is not so much with what the author did, but how he did it. It might be fairly easy to train students to echo Hemingway and to produce one, two, or even thirty Hemingways of the moment. But our concern is with the process rather than the product. Therefore, we do more than imitate; we ask questions about his language, his ideas, his relationships in order to answer: "How did the author achieve his effect?"

The sentence patterns proposed by Wolfe in a recent *English Journal* are a good example of the employment of models for imitation (*4*). The student, by imitating specific sentences, is alerted to the possibilities of their various elements and forced to experiment with them. Thus, through the activity of composition, he is encouraged to increase his own repertoire of sentence structures—perhaps better able to contain the ideas he is waiting to express, and certainly better able to understand the ideas someone else has written. Always we are focusing on the *process* by which ideas are communicated rather than on the product of the effort. Thus, the student gains insight into writing and reading simultaneously.

Forced to wrestle with his own words through generating sentences of his own and imitating models, a student should develop real insights into both the logical and structural devices of coherence. He will learn the use of logical connectives; through actual practice with "moreover," "however," "because," or "since" he will see that their use commits him to the establishment of certain thought relationships. He will also see the relationships signalled by structural connectives. The use of certain structural signals such as "in the beginning," "next," or "later"—or even the more subtle grammatical constructions like parallelism—will make him more aware of these signals when he encounters them in his reading.

---

*From a series of lessons in grammar and sentence building designed by Mearl Dodge and used in his classes in Skokie Junior High School, Winnetka, Illinois.

Ideally, the student should see a picture of what he wishes to write in terms of a lead sentence in a big block at the top and details in smaller blocks attached to the larger block, either coordinately or subordinately; thus, he plots a mental diagram of relationships. Hopefully, as a reader he can then reproduce another writer's diagram.

The same devices for achieving coherence apply whether we are relating sentences within paragraphs or paragraphs within longer pieces of writing. And again the creation of a highly structured series of lessons can help students to understand and practice the relationships involved. As a preliminary overview, the class should be led through the analysis of the structure of a model four or five paragraph theme. The students can then be divided into groups for the writing, evaluating, and revising of a single paragraph. Each group develops a paragraph on a different aspect of the same general topic. Then, in order to see the larger relationships for himself, the student can be given a mimeographed set of each of the group paragraphs and a set of directions by which he can combine the separate paragraphs into a longer theme. Given the individual paragraphs, he must now create a coherent structure which unites them. His directions will guide him through these steps: (1) deciding what over-all theme topic the paragraphs fit; (2) deciding what paragraph order is the most effective; (3) writing an introductory paragraph which accomplishes certain specified goals; (4) re-writing the first sentence of each paragraph to achieve smooth transition; and (5) writing a concluding paragraph which effectively summarizes according to certain specified goals. Since the student does not re-copy the paragraphs themselves, what he has written stands out as the skeleton which shapes a longer communication.

This discussion has thus far been concerned with increasing a student's awareness of structure. Structure in itself, however, is not communication. We must be equally concerned with the details that give structure its meaning, its flesh and blood. Thus we must be equally concerned with the concept of specificity.

The Concept of Specificity

Teachers complain that students' themes say nothing! Students complain that they have nothing to say. They seem to think and write in generalities. Their papers are often like outlines—thoughts remain cold and unprojected and ideas bare and unsupported. Note, for instance, this example.

I don't think I'd like a woman president. I don't think they would be right for the job! What I mean by this is a person suited for the seat of the presidency is one of special talent. A woman may have this talent, sure, but she does not belong as president. My opinion may vary from others but it's mine and like everybody else, "I think I'm right."

This, of course, is glaringly bad, for its idea is completely unsupported. It's an "I Think What I Think Because I Think It" theme.

Here is a part of a paragraph which illustrates another common problem.

It was the first day of hunting season and my father, brother and myself were anxious to get out on the field. We arrived at the farm where we were to hunt that day about six o'clock. After checking the guns we loaded them. We spread out over an area and started walking. Almost at once, a pheasant fell and I reloaded just in time, for just then two more shot up. I got one and my father got the other. All together we got five that day, but I was especially happy because it was the first time I had shot a pheasant. The pheasants tasted especially good at Thanksgiving dinner.

This paragraph is structurally all right but it is run-of-the-mill; it is pedestrian, lacking that come-alive quality a good communication needs. As teachers, we often mark these themes, "Add more concrete details!" But our directions themselves lack the specificity we are asking for. Seldom does a student know how to add more concrete detail and our bare-boned comment doesn't help. How can we help a student to be more concrete and what will it mean for his reading?

Whether our goal is utilitarian prose or narration, the ideas need to be fully supported. Practicing specific methods of support is one way that students can learn to be more concrete. There are many methods of support and there is no one list of methods upon which everyone agrees. Others may find overlappings or omissions, but the following list has served us well:

    (1) general to particular;
    (2) particular to general;
    (3) division or enumeration;
    (4) comparison and contrast;
    (5) details of space or time;
    (6) definition;

(7) cause and effect;

(8) analogy.

Each of these may be considered a method of support for sentences or paragraphs, or even longer themes; and students can examine all in order to make some discoveries. They will undoubtedly discover that occasionally a paragraph is a pure breed, using only a single method of support. More often, however, they will identify several methods of support combined within a single paragraph. They will discover, too, that topic sentences often dictate the kind of support which the paragraph must develop. A student should recognize that a sentence like "Airplane accidents can be related to weather conditions," demands a cause and effect development. If he encounters a sentence like "There are roughly three types of teen-agers," he should be instantly alerted to look for the enumeration of the three kinds.

Such discoveries should be fixed by writing practice. The student himself should write topic sentences which demand a specific method of support. By rewriting the same topic sentences, framing them so that they require different kinds of support. Having worked with various kinds of supports, he is prepared to write paragraphs for which he chooses the method of development that best fits what he wants to say. This writing practice can be reinforced by directing students to readings which themselves follow these methods and by noting that the use of specific kinds of support has given the writer "something to say."

Had the student who objected to a woman for President known that he could support his statement with examples or with comparisons or with a definition of role or with a combination of these, his writing, too, would have gained "something to say."

We have observed in the telling of the hunting episode a thin paragraph. With few details that fatten its meaning, it has little or no impact on the reader. Perhaps the work of Francis Christensen* has application here and will prove an aid not only to our students' writing but to their reading as well. One of the aspects of Christensen's work on the generative rhetoric of the sentence is his work on sentence expansion. There is a certain gift of language which, admittedly, no one can communicate; he

---

*Syntax and the Rhetoric of the Sentence, Grade 9, Student Packet: Experimental Materials, based on the work of Francis Christensen (The University of Nebraska: Nebraska Curriculum Development Center, 1965).

The Rhetoric of Short Units of the Composition, Grade 10, Student Packet: Experimental Materials, based on the work of Francis Christensen (The University of Nebraska: Nebraska Curriculum Development Center, 1965).

believes, however, that specificity and the use of concrete details, and therefore something of style, can and should be taught. He describes three ways in which the thin stream of base words—the nouns and verbs—can be sharpened: by adding a quality, by pointing to some part or detail, by suggesting a likeness to something else. Take the word *field* in the first sentence of our hunting theme. We can sharpen its image by adding (*1*) a quality: *stubbled* field; (*2*) a detail: *field stark against the dawn;* or (*3*) a likeness: *field like a deserted battleground. Arrived* can be sharpened by the same three methods: (1) Add a quality and you have *arrived excitedly;* (2) add a detail and you have *arrived with anticipation;* and (3) add a likeness and you have *arrived silently, like a morning breeze on a quiet summer day.*

Through exercises such as this, a student is forced to draw on sense impressions. We have found controlled exercises on the use of sense impressions, even without the Christensen framework, extremely successful. There is always play with words; use of comparative and imaginative language flowers; and the student is forced to acute observation which might even lead him to a greater awareness of life. Is it not possible that something of this aesthetic sense will be transferred to the study of literature?

Alerting students to specificity through ways that are both practical and imaginative should help to carry them through the poetic descriptions of a Willa Cather; through the sharp images of a John Knowles; the vividness of a McKinlay Kantor; and the emotions of a Brontë or a Browning.

Conclusion

We are not suggesting that it is possible to reduce the thinking skills of writing and reading to a science. We are suggesting only that by developing a careful program that moves step-by-step toward developing the behaviors common to both writing and reading, we can provide a framework through which students can gain facility as consumers as well as producers of a communication.

The bulk of the reading-writing experiences discussed here deals with the skills of exposition. An inspired curriculum, however, will provide just as carefully for literature. It is in this area that we are now focusing attention. Again, the concepts of specificity and structure are central to the units we are planning, for we believe that the more students learn about *how* an author created his work the more they will discover meaning. Again, too, writing and reading lessons are intimately related, for we believe that in the attempt to create or imitate a certain form or genre, students will come to a greater appreciation and understanding of it. In our planning, then, structure is the key; for a knowledge of structure can be transferred from one learning situation to another and thus becomes a tool for further learning.

REFERENCES

1. Andresen, Oliver. "Interrelating Reading and Writing in Grades Nine Through Fourteen," in *Reading and the Language Arts,* compiled and edited by H. Alan Robinson ("Supplementary Educational Monographs," No. 93). Chicago: University of Chicago Press, 1963, 131-137.
2. Robinson, H. Alan. "A Cluster of Skills: Especially for Junior High School," *Reading Teacher,* XV (September 1961), 25-28.
3. Whitehead, Alfred North. *The Aims of Education.* New York: The New American Library of World Literature, Inc., 1929, A Mentor Paperback, 39-50.
4. Wolfe, Don M. "Grammar and Linguistics: A Contrast in Realities," *English Journal,* LIII (February 1964), 73-78.

OLIVER ANDRESEN

ILLINOIS STATE TEACHERS COLLEGE, CHICAGO SOUTH

6. Evaluating the Author's Theme in Literature

ACCORDING TO CHASE, the inability of many readers today to read reflectively is a "higher illiteracy."* In other words, such readers are unable to relate the world of ideas which they encounter in print to the real world of their own experiences.

*Francis S. Chase. "In the Next Decade," *Controversial Issues in Reading and Promising Solutions* (edited by Helen M. Robinson). Chicago: University of Chicago Press, 1961, p. 7-18.

Chase is not speaking, in this instance, of people who have basic reading problems. He is concerned with students and with alumni of the American system of education who know how to read and, perhaps, even want to; and yet these students do not read material of high quality with sufficient understanding or reflection. As a result, such readers remain impoverished for enlightenment concerning themselves and the world around them.

Is Chase's thesis valid? Do the literacy programs of our high schools produce victims of "higher illiteracy?"

In an effort to appraise the amount as well as the calibre of independent reading of students in a Chicago suburban high school, the head of the English Department submitted a questionnaire to these students with the following direction: "List below the books that you have read once and would enjoy reading again."

Few English department chairmen in our schools today would be surprised at the responses. For the most part, students listed only those books which they had been required to read in class. *Ivanhoe, The Scarlet Letter,* and *Gulliver's Travels* were prominent among the choices. Included also were titles of individual short stories, along with titles of current movies and, in one case, *The Chicago Tribune* was listed.

Supposedly, the purpose of the literature program in American high schools is dual in nature. High school students should not only become acquainted with a few great literary works, but hopefully will also become so stimulated as to pursue more literature of equal quality for the rest of their lives. This pursuit is certainly considered a basic characteristic of an "educated" American.

Consequently, two trends were looked for among the data accrued by this questionnaire. First, did students, who enjoyed a particular literary selection in class, search for and find other work by the same author to read independently? Second, did students tend to "catch fire" with a particular topic brought forth by the study of a literary work and therefore search out other writing on that topic?

In a small number of cases these trends were evident. For example, some students after reading J. D. Salinger's *Catcher in the Rye* as a class assignment, did follow, on their own, with *Frannie and Zooey*. Or some students followed *Catcher in the Rye* with other books concerning the world of the teenager, such as John Knowles' *A Separate Peace*.

In fact, the analysis of specific topics pursued independently proved to be most enlightening. One would expect high school boys, who read independently, to dwell on such topics as sports cars or athletics and expect girls to spend their leisure time reading books of high romance. Indeed, these topics were evident; but they were not the most prevalent. The data revealed that the number one topic to be pursued in independent reading for this particular high school was that of religion. The second was that of racial issues. The third was concerned with general teenage social adjustment. Apparently then, some teenagers do look to good literature for an explanation of the world around them and for insight into themselves. Such readers are not victims of higher illiteracy. Yet, despite the aims of literature programs, the number of these enlightened readers is small. Why?

Science Versus Spirit

We are all very much impressed these days with the fact that the genius of man has turned the old frontiers of science into thresholds of new understanding. Commander White's walk in space annihilated many misconceptions concerning the dangers of celestial travel which until now have inhibited a future landing on the moon. At the same time, scientific discoveries in the area of genetics are leading to the unraveling of the mysteries of heredity. Yet, behind this intellectual progress lies the promise that these scientific concepts, now coming to light, within ten years will be as obsolete as yesterday's scrub board.

Because of the excitement engendered by these "breakthroughs" in science and because of the rivalry now rampant among international ideologies to enhance prestige through scientific achievements, academic institutions throughout the world are crowding their curriculums with courses of mathematics, natural science, physics, and chemistry. Interspersed among these subjects are those of engineering, electronics, and the mechanical arts. Indeed, man with accelerating speed presses to understand the flesh of which he is made and the clay upon which he lives.

Yet, even a child senses that there is another side of man. Along with the power of his reason there is the depth of his feeling. Along with the hunger of his mind for understanding of the universe, there is the thirst of his spirit for an understanding of himself. In our age, man is glutting his mind with knowledge of the world while his spirit is starving for insight.

This dearth of insight is serious. In our time poliomyelitis can be wiped from the earth; yet, no one knows why the German nation went insane and ravaged the world like a plague to the price of half a billion souls. Mars has been found to be a dead world; yet, no one can determine a universally acceptable purpose for life on our planet. The American people are the most opulent and healthy in history; yet, suicide is a leading disease among our youth.

The Need for the Study of Literature

The questions raised by man in search of understanding about himself cannot be delegated by educators solely to the attention of philosophers and to the church. If education is to prepare young people for the future demands of life, then education must teach students to fulfill spiritual as well as physical needs.

The laboratory in which man studies the problems of his spirit is the medium of art. Through art, man tries to solve the riddles of love and loneliness, of life and death. Man continually changes his environment in order to alleviate problems concerning his physical needs. As a result, his tools grow obsolete, his shelters become more complex, his cities are altered, his civilizations crumble and are forgotten. But man, as yet, has discovered very little about how to alleviate the problems of his spirit. Consequently, the artifices through which he has discourse on these problems do not lose their meaning.

Perhaps the most significant medium through which man speaks directly to himself is literature. Most of this dialogue is banal; yet, within each generation there are, perhaps, a dozen minds of such brilliance and understanding that what they add to this dialogue is of universal importance. Because these artists speak through literature, their thinking is immortal. As the centuries have rolled by, this vast storehouse of understanding has increased a thousand fold. According to Somerset Maugham, a man would need over two and a half life spans of constant reading to read all of the world's significant books.

A tragedy of our day is that many students hardly attend to this type of reading. Indeed, publishers are waxing fat over the current upsurge of the book market; yet, the literary quality of most of this material is questionable. Much of it lacks artistic expression and the thinking manifested is insipid. Rather than generating insight within the reader, most best sellers today misguide and confuse him.

Educators commonly react to this situation with the comment that many students have neither the intelligence nor the imagination to read good books. To some extent, perhaps, this opinion is true. Yet, this writer would rather listen to the laments of the students themselves for the answer. What teacher of literature has not heard a bright student reply, after reading for a moment, "I don't get it." Such a student does not mean that he cannot recognize the words nor that he cannot grasp what the author is telling him. What he does mean is that he does not perceive what the author is *saying*. In other words, he cannot see the application of the author's theme to his own experience. No wonder! When has he been taught specific skills by which to see what the author means as well as what he tells?

Is not a great part of the problem, then, one of teaching literary appreciation? Do the current methods of teaching literature give a student skill with which to guide his mind towards understanding, interpretation, and integration of the ideas within a good book?

Methods of Teaching Literature

For the past three years this writer has had the opportunity to observe a great many literature classes at high school level. For the most part, these classes contained students who had at least average intelligence and who, according to reading survey tests, could read at least with the expected proficiency of their age and class. Yet, most of these students read only under academic compulsion.

During his observation, this writer noted three types of teaching methods generally used in the presentation of literary selections. For example, he remembers one teacher standing before the class with an anthology opened to a selection by Thoreau. "What does that mean?" she asked repeatedly, as the students dragged their minds from one mid-nineteenth century phrase to another. Progress was difficult, tiresome, and slow. With the ringing of the bell this teacher promptly shut her book —although only approximately a column and a half of the selection had been covered—and announced to the class, "That ends Thoreau. Now, tomorrow we will take up Emerson." What skills for reading literature had this class learned during the hour? Apparently, they had accomplished little else than the translation of some nineteenth century idioms. Yet, such a teaching technique, exemplified by this teacher's presentation, appeared to this writer to be one of the most common procedures used for the teaching of literature.

Another teacher comes to this writer's mind. A teacher with an opened anthology against her ample breast repeatedly asked, "Then what happened? And then what?" Only three of the twenty-five students in the class were responding, each attempting to outdo the others in unfolding the plot of the selection under discussion. The other twenty-two students talked quietly with one another or stared into space. What literary reading skill was being presented in this class? Apparently, the ability to follow sequences or the ability to anticipate an outcome were being developed— but little else. Yet, according to this writer's observation, the "Then what?" method seems to be the next most common in the teaching of literature.

When discussing assigned reading for a literature class, some teachers would ask such questions as, "Do you like Scarlet O'Hara? Would you like her as a friend?" These teachers at least would be giving their students experience in character analysis, a skill which comes close to the purpose of studying literature.

Very seldom during his observations did this writer encounter a teacher who directed his students towards understanding the author's theme. In other words, seldom did students understand that the selections being studied were works of art. Seldom did the students realize that as works of art, these selections had personal explanations of life circumstances. And regrettably, when a theme was discovered little was done with it other than to classify it under one of the three standard and meaningless categories: Man versus Man, Man versus Nature, and Man versus

Himself. No attempt was made to guide the student into integrating the theme into his own experience.

Not only do these methods allow the students to pass over much of the richness that can be gained through vicarious experiences through literature, they also have another basic weakness. They add nothing to the student's ability to evaluate anything he reads. Such methods guide him towards some understanding of a specific selection only. He is left with nothing in his mind that will encourage him to read on his own and that will help him to pass intelligent judgment on what he reads independently.

Therefore, methods for teaching literature are needed which will build within the student's mind a specific approach for content analysis. Such an approach must be independent of any particular literary selection and therefore applicable to all literary selections. Certainly no two students, using the same method of literary analysis, are going to arrive at the same level of appreciation or at the same degree of understanding of any literary selection—any more than two golfers, using the same techniques, will develop the same proficiency in the game. Yet, these readers if taught a method to analyze literature—just as the golfers if taught specific techniques—will pursue their endeavors with greater discrimination and enthusiasm.

During the course of his experience, this writer has designed several such structures which can be used as a guide for content analysis of literature. He is not convinced that any of the structures of his invention are the answer to the needs of literary instruction; but he has found through his own experience and through experimentation that one such structure, at least, is helpful. A description of this structure will be presented here to serve not so much as a suggested method in itself but as a model by which teachers of literature might design such teaching methods of their own.

The Profundity Scale

The particular structure this writer has in mind is the Profundity Scale. This scale consists of five points or levels (arbitrarily determined); and its purpose is to serve the reader as a "tool" by which he can not only ferret out the author's theme but also evaluate its degree of profundity.

High school students readily understand the concept of *depth* in reference to people. They attribute to this quality such characteristics as wisdom, seriousness, and maturity. With some guidance they can understand that a *deep* teenager is one who nearly possesses the qualities of the "universal" wise and understanding adult. A shallow teenager, on the other hand, is one who is silly, self-centered, and childish. At the same time, high school students realize that in the course of human history occasionally there are teachers or philosophers endowed with such wisdom that they understand the problems basic to all men of anytime, anywhere, throughout the universe. Examples of such teachers are Solomon, Buddha, Socrates, and St. Augustine. The minds of such men are concerned with the fundamental truths about man, not only in this world but in the possible worlds to come.

From a discussion concerning the profundity of people, students can then be led to understand the concept of the profundity of ideas. Those ideas concerned with the trivia of any particular person's day tend to be shallow. Those ideas concerned with the universal aspects of all mens' lives are profound. Profundity, then, can be defined as the degree towards universality at which an idea pertains to the nature of all mankind.

Generally speaking, an artist is a person of such sensitivity that through his art he can give his public insight into their own natures, and into the dynamics of the world about them. Specifically, an author gives his interpretations through the themes in his writing.

To perceive this insight in a literary work and to incorporate it into his own experience, the reader must first determine the author's theme and then pass judgment on it in light of the reader's personal experience and understanding.

The Profundity Scale, then, is an abstract structure by which the reader can discover, interpret, and perhaps integrate the author's theme into his own experience. The five levels of the Profundity Scale are as follows:

The lowest or least profound level is the *Physical Plane*. A story which operates primarily on the physical plane leads the reader to be concerned with the physical actions of the characters. Slapstick comedy is not much above this level. The author primarily intends to give the reader entertainment through vicarious physical action. Fiction of this nature, although fun, gives the reader little insight into life.

The second level is the *Mental Plane*. At this level the reader is concerned not only with the physical actions of the characters, but with their mental actions as well. A stereotyped detective story is an example of literature at this level. Such a story gives the reader somewhat more understanding and insight into life than would a slapstick comedy.

The next most profound level is the *Moral Plane*. At this level, the reader is led to be concerned not only with the characters' physical and mental actions but with their moral actions as well. An example would be a story in which a character wrestles with his conscience according to a moral code. If the theme of a story on this plane tends to dove-tail with a problem of a particular reader, an insight into his problem might be gained.

The fourth level is the *Psychological Plane*. At this level, the reader attends not only to the characters' physical, mental, and moral actions but to the "why" of the actions. In other words, the story presents a realistic environment and shows the effects of this environment on the characters operating within it. An example of such a story is Willa Cather's "Paul's Case," the story of a sensitive teenager driven to crime and suicide because of the ugliness of his environment. A good story at this level can give readers considerable understanding of a particular class or society.

The fifth and most profound level is the *Philosophical Plane*. At this level, the reader attends not only to the characters' physical, mental, moral, and psychological actions but to the aspects of these characters which tend to be universal for all men. In other words, these characters are so richly drawn that they would be recognizable to anyone, anywhere, any time in history. The resulting theme is therefore also universal. It can engender insight in almost any reader regardless of his own experience. An example of such a character is Macbeth who, in his soliloquy "Tomorrow and tomorrow and tomorrow," proclaims the emptiness of life before the fact of death—a feeling of despair everyone can experience at least once in a lifetime.

Students can be led to understand the five levels of the Profundity Scale by comparing them to the various levels of a friendship. The first aspect one becomes acquainted with in meeting a new friend is his physical appearance. But the association is hardly very "deep" at this point of development. After some conversation, however, one begins to appraise the mind of his new acquaintance. As the association continues, one then begins to know the moral standards or ethics of his friend. After one becomes acquainted with the environment in which his friend has lived, an understanding—to some degree at least—of the dynamics behind the new friend's behavior is developed. Finally, as the friendship ripens through the years, one understands more and more the relationship of the friend's life to the overall pattern of all men's lives.

Using the Profundity Scale

Students will see the purpose of the Profundity Scale as an evaluating instrument when it is applied to various types of drama on television. "The Three Stooges," a slap-stick comedy, for example, does not say very much beyond the Physical Plane. True, this program has a theme, namely that "dumb guys" are funny; but such a theme is too ridiculous for serious consideration. A more profound type of program is "The Sherlock Holmes Theatre." In such a drama the reader is primarily concerned with the cleverness of the characters and can find some satisfaction in the theme that cleverness can bring about justice; yet, after some thought, this theme can, in many respects, be declared invalid.

Currently, a television series with very high ratings is portraying the virtues and debaucheries of "folks" in a small New England town. The theme, the dual nature of man, indeed, might lead the obtuse viewer to accept the good and the bad sides of his own or someone else's character; yet, a drama speaking at this level gives little interpretation of the dynamics behind the behavior of its characters. Consequently, viewers gain little insight into their own or their associates' behavior.

Occasionally, a drama on television will tell the story of characters in a particular community or society, pointing out the influences of the environment on the behavior of its members. The theme of such a program, generally speaking, is that many people are molded by their surroundings and associates. This can lead the viewer to considerable insight into his own behavior as well as that of the people he must deal with.

Rarely on television is a drama presented with characters so well drawn that they portray, with clarity, qualities basic in everyone. Such characters "come alive." An example would be the remarkable program, now extinct because of low ratings, entitled "The Play of the Week." This writer remembers a particularly brilliant production of Eugene O'Neil's *The Iceman Cometh*, the story of people heavily engrossed in the terrors of their own weaknesses only to find that the hero, the one man who could make them happy, had destroyed his wife because he could no longer stand her tolerance of his inadequacies. So sensitively and sympathetically has the author portrayed these characters that in watching the play a perceiving viewer is led to a better understanding of the fears within himself. Such understanding as this is the basic purpose for the study of literature.

A student cannot search for these various levels in a theme, if he has not been taught to do so. For example, within the last three-hundred years the story *Robinson Crusoe* has had a spell-binding effect on every generation of young readers. In the seventeenth century, a French school teacher commented in his diary that most of his charges had left school for the holidays, each with a copy of *Robinson Crusoe* under a left elbow. The same procession with this book could happen today. Obviously, a book with such enduring magnetism has a universal theme. Yet, many readers, who might nevertheless enjoy it, do not know how to grasp its complete worth.

For example, this writer remembers one particular young man who replied after being urged to read the book, "Gee Sir, this is a great story. I sure liked all that stuff about the shipwreck and the shooting of all them cannibals." Unfortunately, although the boy perhaps sensed that he was dealing with an extraordinary book, he was incapable of seeing its significance much beyond the physical level.

Again several young scholars have told the writer that they loved *Robinson Crusoe* because its hero was so clever in devising tools for agriculture and weapons for defense. Regardless of their enthusiasm, these young readers were still unable to perceive the depths about life that could be communicated to them by this work. Their understanding of this classic reached only to the mental plane because they did not know how to look for any deeper meaning.

In all probability Defoe meant the tale to be a moralistic lesson—the story of a young man who defied his parents by running away to sea only to encounter disaster. Most modern editions omit the lengthy discourse on this matter altogether.

Defoe, of course, lived two centuries before the great Sigmund Freud. Nevertheless, because he was a genius with a unique understanding of the human mind, he portrayed a fascinating account of a character grappling with the hostile forces of a foreign environment. This portrayal is particularly unique considering the fact that many of the conditions a tropical island so described are not altogether accurate. Few if any tropical islands have wild goats. Nevertheless, the problems at this level are realistically presented. Crusoe approaches madness before he can adjust to his strange environs. A reader who can perceive the discussion in the book at this psychological level would gain a great deal of insight into his own reactions to strange situations.

Defoe gave this book immortality by his extraordinary presentation of a man's struggle with "aloneness." Crusoe was more than lonely. He was alone—cut off from all intercourse with man. Is not this a basic fear in all men? Why else is a delinquent quickly brought to bay when threatened with solitary confinement? Why does a child refuse to be left alone at night? Why else does man fear death? A perceptive person reading *Robinson Crusoe* at the philosophical level, will not only gain insight into his own fears of aloneness but also, with this insight, better appreciate the people around him.

A student who understands the nature and the purposes of the Profundity Scale, then, usually can begin to seek out these deeper meanings for himself. As a result, he can formulate questions in his mind, concerning these five levels until he has determined the full scope of what the author is saying. A discussion in class based on the Profundity Scale will reinforce his endeavors. After such experiences as this in the classroom, the student begins to see literature as a composite rather than as bits and pieces of things scattered throughout a thousand anthologies. He employs a method in his approach to literature; he now knows what he wants from his reading and, most likely, will end up achieving what he is after.

Need for Other Structures

Evaluating an author's theme is only one aspect of the complex process of literary appreciation. Analysis of characters, settings, and style, is also necessary. An inventive teacher might devise structures for any one of these elements of literature. For example, one might categorize characters from "good guys—bad guys" through the "unique" person to a universal symbol of greed or nobility. Or one might categorize settings from rhetorical description through sensory imagery to mood and then, perhaps, to a universal aura.

The arbitrary labeling of the various points in the continuum of any one of these elements is not so important. That the students, particularly problem readers, can be given some kind of abstract structure or framework which they can carry in their minds from one literary selection to another is the significant thing. The reason is that with these structures students can guide their minds to the best of what the author has to offer them. And once they are able to recognize great writing and to evaluate its greatness, such students most likely will pass with eagerness into a state of higher literacy where the thinking of some of the greatest minds that have inhabited the earth is waiting for them.

MARION D. JENKINSON

UNIVERSITY OF ALBERTA

7. Increasing Reading Power in Social Studies

SOCIAL STUDIES, embracing many different branches of human activity, and being concerned with the "there and then," as well as the "here and now," involves a range of content unequaled in any other subject area. Consequently, the reading matter which conveys the concepts is equally varied in terms of words, ideas and modes of thinking.

Though, undoubtedly, comprehension is enhanced by the amount of "meanings" from his experience background which a student brings *to* the printed page, if he is to learn through reading he must derive *meaning* from it also.

Comprehension involves the ability to interact appropriately with small units such as words as well as larger units such as phrases, sentences and paragraphs. The reading process demands a perception of these words or larger units, the production of associations, the selection of the relevant ones, and a synthesis of these to produce meaning. This indicates that reading involves a "divergent" production of calling up associations and a "convergent" production of selecting and synthesizing the relevant ones. Any word calls up a number of associations, but the word is limited in its meaning by the sentence and passage in which it is used. Similarly, a sentence and even an entire paragraph may be restricted in meaning by its context. Thus, the meaning of a passage is partially gained by the meaning of the words themselves, and partially by their rearrangement in a specific structure. This would imply that reading not only demands an ability to perceive ideas, but also an ability to limit and arrange these ideas according to the structure of the entire passage.

Hence, if we are to increase reading power in social studies, two major considerations are the development of functional word knowledge and of strategies for understanding material in this content field.

Functional Word Knowledge

The importance of understanding the words and terms appropriate to each topic has long been recognized as essential in the reading of social studies material (*1*). Stress has been laid upon the necessity for ensuring breadth and depth of meaning so that the concepts underlying the words are realized to the full (*5*). There is some evidence, however, that both teachers of reading and subject area specialists concentrate upon the words which are peculiar to the different content areas. Yet there appear to be three areas of word knowledge which reading teachers should be emphasizing: function words, shifts of word meaning, and classifying through word meaning.

Function Words

The understanding of the "small" words, those words the Chinese call "empty" words but which are indispensable to any language, should be developed systematically. The so-called coordinators or connectives separated by themselves, have little meaning, but in context often carry the major burden of precise meaning. Too often, they are regarded as merely rhetorical guides, whereas many of them, in fact, give the whole direction to thinking. The provision of experience and direct teaching of the meaning of the correlatives such as "both" . . . "and," "not" . . . "only," "but" . . . "also," "either" . . . "or" is vital. Again we can utilize examples from the pupil's own reading and also give them exercises directed specifically towards their use. So with the structure words that suggest:

(1) cause and effect—"because," "since," "so that,"
(2) those which suggest condition—"if," "unless," "although,"
(3) those that indicate contrast—"whereas," "while,"
(4) those that state time relationships—"as," "before," "when," "after," "during," "while," etc.,
(5) those which introduce parallel ideas—"however," "therefore," "nevertheless," "hence," "accordingly," "similarly," "on the other hand," "in conclusion," and so on.

It is interesting to note that there are several words that have multiple meanings. For instance, "while" may indicate a time relationship, or a condition, or introduce a parallel idea. Lack of confusion as to the appropriate meaning in the specific context is essential for accurate comprehension.

Starting from the student's own experience we should make him aware of the differences. Take, for example, time relation words used in the following sentences.

1. (a) While Mr. West walked across the room he read a book.
   (b) Mr. West walked across the room reading a book.
   (c) Mr. West walked across the room and read a book.
   (d) Mr. West read a book as he walked across the room.
2. (a) When Mr. West moved quietly on tiptoe he approached the door.
   (b) Mr. West moved quietly on tiptoe and then approached the door.
   (c) After Mr. West had been moving quietly on tiptoe for a little while, he approached the door.
   (d) Moving quietly on tiptoe, Mr. West approached the door.
3. (a) Stooping down and keeping his knees stiff, Mr. West found that he was just able to touch his toes.
   (b) When he had stooped as far as he could, Mr. West found that, keeping his knees stiff, he was just able to touch his toes.
   (c) Having kept his knees stiff, Mr. West stooped down and found that he was just able to touch his toes.
   (d) When he began to stoop down Mr. West kept his knees stiff and found that he was just able to touch his toes.

Students might be asked to demonstrate the related actions by mime before explaining them verbally. It is interesting to note that though the sentences in the third section appear to be longer and more complicated, these are usually easier to understand than the shorter, more concise sentences in section one. Here meaning is embedded in "while," the use of the present participle reading, "and," and "as." This apparent simplicity of sentence structure frequently overlays complexity of thought.

These "empty" words then suggest to the reader the way in which he should structure his thinking. They are important in any formal writing, but perhaps are used most frequently in social studies material. Time and space concepts as well as the need to explain the multiple motives of human development, the manifold cause and effect relationships of past events as well as current phenomena, and the inter-dependence of economic development, are the essence of this subject. And it is perhaps a paradox that this very complexity can only be conveyed if there is precise and penetrating understanding of these "small" structure words.

Shifts in Word Meaning

An oft reiterated truism is that readers should learn to understand

words in use. The extent to which technical vocabulary of subject fields
conditions learning in these fields has also been discussed frequently. But
students continue to ignore the shifts of meaning that occur as words occur
in different context. Two major stumbling blocks in social studies appear
to be the use of familiar words in unfamiliar context, and the metaphorical
implications of terms. Many words, with which the student has become
familiar during the elementary school period, now are joined into terms.
In terms such as "machine age," it is not sufficient that the student knows
the meaning of "machine" and "age." He cannot add the meaning of
one word to another but must abstract ideas from the concepts underlying
these words and synthesize these into a new concept. Think of the
transition in thought required from "west" to "westward movement" or
from that type of "movement" to "labor movement." Far too frequently
we hopefully assume that if the student can "recognize" a word, he has
understood its meaning. Students, particularly those who have difficulties
in reading, need help with these shifts of meaning. Many of them may
associate "density of population" with the intelligence of a group of
people, or confine the meaning of "cabinet" or "minister" to their own
experience and associate these with furniture or clergymen.

Social studies material abounds with metaphorical expressions. Teachers
who do not allow students to ponder the implicit meanings of these
phrases, will not only inhibit vocabulary but will impoverish the social
studies concepts. Discussion of such terms as the "iron curtain," or "the
cold war," can be illuminating. Could a curtain be made of iron? What
ideas does this juxtaposition of opposites evoke? Why do we speak of a
tariff *wall?* What is the origin of the term "Tropic of Cancer"?
Fascinating discussions may arise not only about the word origins of
"cancer," but also the linking of astronomy and astrology by the early
cartographers. Teachers should never miss the opportunity to explore such
terms; they will often be surprised at the insights which can be developed.

Classifying Word Meanings

One of the major ways in which we can aid thinking through language
is by using words to aid in the classification of ideas. Most learning takes
place through the recognition of similarities and differences. Perhaps we
need to explore the possibilities of direct classification through this method.

The precise nature of the following terms could be discovered through
discussion:

How is democracy like a republic?

How is a democracy different from a republic?
Can a republic be a kingdom?
Can a kingdom be a democracy?

or

How is a declaration like a proclamation?
How is a declaration different from a proclamation?
Can a declaration be a proclamation?

Discussion which goes beyond the superficial and sometimes vague apprehension of the meaning of a word in context is essential to increasing the ability to understand and to the transfer of knowledge from one occasion to another. Too frequently, discussion of such topics is regarded by teachers as a waste of time and leads frequently to incomplete and partial concepts. Astute questioning by the teacher, however, can lead not only to vocabulary extension but also to precision in thinking.

Research in the development of children's thinking suggests that the ability to apprehend overlapping classifications develops only slowly and is barely achieved by the time children enter high school. Again our work in vocabulary might foster this increasing awareness of complexity. The following exercise of "paired qualities" might be used as a starting point.

Paired Qualities

1. The same person could be both *kind* and *gentle*.
2. The same person could be both *handsome* and *ugly*.
3. The same place could be both *precipitous* and *a plateau*.
4. The land could be both *fertile* and *arid*.
5. The climate could be both *humid* and *dank*.
6. A person could regard the same event as both *calamitous* and *felicitous*.

Students should be encouraged to formulate their own pairs. This is merely another way of teaching the dichotomies of thinking involved when we work with antonyms, and the similarity but not identity of synonyms.

From experiences such as these, we can then attempt to increase the ability of students to formulate their own accurate precise definitions. There is some evidence, from research in vocabulary development in later grades, that children today are not as accurate in this skill as formerly.

Further work in classification of ideas through word usage might help students to understand not only *what* an author is saying but *how* he is saying it. Again it would appear easier to start from the students' own experiences. Most test questions, which demand that a student organize his answers, have clues that indicate the nature and content of the answer. Thus the words "describe," "illustrate," and "outline" imply that the answer requires only that ideas are so ordered as to present the most accurate and most comprehensive communication. When we ask students "to give reasons for," "explain," "account for," "analyze," "elucidate," or "interpret" we are demanding another type of response. Here the criterion is that there should be at least an acknowledgement of the cause and effect relationship, and that the answers should be organized to indicate the interrelation of ideas or events. The use of the imperatives "compare" and "contrast" is also interesting. "Compare" implies use of both similarities and differences, while "contrast" focuses attention on the differences. However, when we use terms such as "evaluate," "consider," "criticize," "examine," or "comment upon," the highest of the mental processes involved in comprehension are demanded. These include such abilities as analyzing, judging, synthesizing, induction, deduction, generalizing, and problem solving.

It is obvious, however, that at this stage we are reaching into an area of general comprehension as well as specific word meanings. So let us examine some strategies in comprehending social studies material.

Comprehension Strategies for Social Studies Material

"Structure" and "strategy" have become popular words in education. Some would say they have degenerated into slogans and their initial meanings have been dissipated. However, the strategies which can be applied in plumbing the structures of thought and language underlying the content of the material appear to offer many suggestions for ensuring comprehensive comprehension. Two areas appear to be within the scope of this chapter—strategies in teaching, and strategies for studying.

Teaching Strategies

Unfortunately the means by which a student arrives at the main idea is frequently left to chance or a random process of elimination. Students who read well usually achieve this by means of an "educated guess." Less able students may need to be given the means by which they can obtain the main idea.

The topic sentence often is the main clue to the meaning of a paragraph. There are three possible positions for this. It may be the introductory sentence, and the remainder of the ideas within the paragraph support or extend the introductory notion. It may be the summary sentence, with all the preceding concepts in the paragraph culminating in the final sentence. These two types of organization illustrate deductive and inductive thinking. Frequently, however, the topic sentence is situated in the middle of the paragraph, with pertinent ideas preceding it and appropriate examples following it.

Sometimes, however, paragraphs contain no topic sentences which give clues to meaning. The main idea may be only gathered implicitly; or the paragraph may be a transitional one, the purpose of which is to make the bridge from one thought to another. McCallister (3) has suggested further clues to the understanding of paragraphs.

At the University of Alberta, we have had considerable success in inducing growth in this ability through diagramming idea sequences in a paragraph. Now while this method has been found to be successful with all types of material, social studies content seems to be particularly amenable to this technique, perhaps because the style is largely explanatory and consequently involves inductive and deductive operations to explain the interrelationships of the ideas.

A productive means of developing competence in comprehension is through discussion with the students of their errors and mistakes. The reader must learn to know himself; his own attitudes, the probable types of mistakes he will make, the pitfalls of language, and the fallacies that may become the booby traps of thinking.

The nature of the content of social studies makes it particularly felicitous from this point of view. Examples abound of the types and sources of errors.

Words, phrases and sentences may be wrongly *interpreted* because of one of the following:

1. "Glittering generalities" (the term used by propaganda analysts),
2. Vagueness and ambiguity,
3. Equivocation and false reference,
4. Jargon, and etymological fallacies,
5. Syntactic and accent ambiguity.

Failure may also occur because the reader does not see the *relationships* among the *ideas* aroused by the words. Three aspects of these are:

(1) Failure to analyze the problem or topic in order to discover the principles, or persons, or points of conflict involved.
(2) Failure to recognize the "pattern" of the problem and the method of presentation, which may be descriptive, critical, legal, exposi-

tory, creative, artistic, and so on.

(3) Failure to assess the basic hypothesis, which may be impractical or not feasible, or irrelevant. A multiplicity of hypotheses may preclude any formulation of a conclusion.

Errors which occur in reading interpretation through faulty logic are almost innumerable. Some of the most prominent ones are:

(1) Generalization on the basis of insufficient or unrepresentative instances.

(2) Ignoring contradictory instances and failure to make them fit in with the total conclusion.

(3) Statistical fallacies (an important aspect in the modern age). These would include drawing inferences about individuals from the measures of a group, imputing causal significance to correlations, non-representative sampling, neglecting to assess the method of collecting statistical data, and to test the consistency of data; and assuming falsely that all other variables except those measured and compared, remain constant, and many more.

Many of the fallacies of classical logic are broadly deductive and consist in drawing inferences which are not justified by the assumptions nor by the generalizations. Some of these which often confuse the reader are:

(1) False assumptions are made or implied by either the author or reader.

(2) Exceptions are overvalued or ignored.

(3) Begging the question by assuming (wrongly) the conclusion is proved, or by so framing a question that a direct answer involves admission of the assumption.

(4) Introduction of irrelevant argument for the purpose of confusing thinking. All the classical types occur here.

(a) You're another.

(b) Argument against the man.

(c) Appeal to popular prejudice.

(d) Appeal to reverence or authority or prestige.

(e) Appeal to pity.

(f) Appeal to the purse.

(5) Introduction of non-sequiturs.

(6) Misuse of analogy.

Finally in our present age of mass communication there are rhetorical devices for confusing thought, particularly group thought. Some of these most commonly used are:

(1) Engendering confusion by the use of evasion, or slogans and cliches, special pleading and the use of statements of doubtful propositions.

(2) Attempting to divert attention from the central thought through the use of the "red herring" and evasive speculation concerning a parallel rather than an actual situation.

(3) Various methods of delaying or blocking, such as gradualism, academic detachment, aggressive raising of objections, repeated affirmation; and the arbitrary, dogmatic appeal to prejudice, should all be recognized for what they are.

If students could recognize some of the sources of their errors they would have embarked along the road to becoming critical readers. In Dryden's phrase they would have learned "the art of judging well."

The content of social studies also demands differing thought responses from the reader. Literature forces the reader to use his imagination, while the logical stimulus of scientific writing requires a corresponding logical response. A wide variety of content is included in social studies and the reader must call into play a wide range of modes of response. These may be guided by chronological, psychological, as well as logical considerations. The ability to project oneself in time and space, the use of imagination demanded by history and geography, must be curbed by "loyalty to the given," or the facts as we know them.

Materials which will give the student practice in detecting thinking strategies and will lead to a self-critical attitude on the part of the student towards his own thought processes do not need to be devised. Examples of all these will be found in most of the materials currently used in social studies.

Strategies for Studying

A recent investigation (4) which examined the development of logical ability and reading comprehension has implications for the teaching of study skills, particularly that of outlining. Perhaps students need to become more flexible in the ways in which they utilize and store knowledge, so that the method more closely approximates the structure of thinking involved in the learning of some concept.

It has been suggested that the familiar linear format recommended for outlining is not always satisfactory.

Title

1. ....
   A.
   B.
   C.
   D.

2. ....
   A.
   B.
   C.
   D.

3. ....
   A.
   B.
   C.
   D.

In this type of outline, item 1 or 2 may be given and the student left to supply the remaining items and sub-items. There appears to be several disadvantages to this type of procedure. The items included in the outline tend to be at a low level of abstraction, and often are merely a listing of details. Moreover, in a linear sequence of this kind it is difficult to indicate relationships, particularly that of inclusion. What is the relationship between 1, 2, and 3 and between A, B, and C. Finally this type of structure may be uneconomical from the point of view of recall. It is important that associative links be made and these are often most effective if they are a result of classification and art part of an organized structure.

Elsewhere (2) it has been suggested that there are sequential steps which might be used to develop different methods of organization which follow the steps in the developing logic of children. Such diagrams go from linear sequences, to correlated sequences, to parallel sequences, to hierarchical sequence and ultimately come to fruition perhaps in a three-dimensional type of matrix.

By grade seven, many children are capable of thinking in terms of hierarchies. The following diagram illustrates how this diagram scheme might be applied to social studies material.

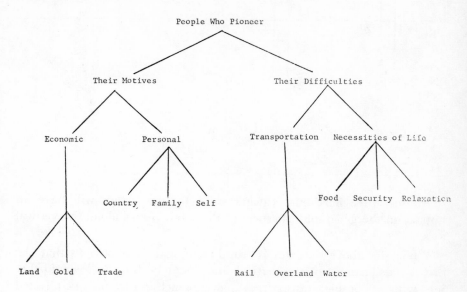

The findings of psychology, however, reveal that all classificatory thinking is *not* hierarchical in form. Classes may be multiplicative in structure and be better indicated by a matrix type of plan, which can indicate more complex relationships. The following diagram suggests a possible use of this form.

	Climate	Physical Features	Natural Resources
H A B I T A T			
P R O D U C T S			

| T |
| R |
| A |
| N |
| S |
| P |
| O |
| R |
| T |

All the three horizontal categories singly or together will have an impact on the geographical aspect of the sub-divisions along the vertical axis.

While the above diagram is two-dimensional, it is obvious that the broad classifications of the vertical line might be broken down further into types of housing, transport, etc., all of which in turn may be affected by features along the horizontal line in terms of climate, physical features, natural resources, as well as in terms of the remainder of the items on the vertical axis. Thus, students could easily produce a three-dimensional model.

It might be argued that texts used in science and social studies have long incorporated information presented in similar diagrammatic form. It has also long been emphasized that we should direct our teaching towards the accurate reading of such charts. I would submit, however, that rarely do we ask the students to do the reverse and record the information they gain from the texts in this way. Given the opportunity and encouragement, many students reveal considerable ingenuity and enterprise in devising means for categorizing their learning.

One word about what we have been doing in the past. The linear format suggested earlier has certain uses, and should not be discarded completely. It has a definite use, whether thinking is linear in terms of a time sequence or where information is additive in nature. It may also be the first step which the teacher has to introduce before the pupil can be led to understand the relevance of hierarchical and matrix structures. We should be doing a great disservice if we assumed that automatically the students would recognize this hierarchical type of organization as being more functional, unless their previous training had led them to this conclusion.

JENKINSON 87

Conclusion

In this paper an attempt has been made to show some specific ways in which the teacher can assist the student in increasing his power of reading in social studies. Many of the aspects of reading in this field, such as adapting rate and method of attack according to the nature of the material and the purpose of the reader and similar ideas, have been omitted because these have been discussed extensively in the literature. It would seem, however, that the processes of reading involve not only imagery, vocabulary, concepts, manipulation *and* understanding of grammatical structure, but are also dependent upon basic logical operations which develop slowly throughout the elementary school but are reaching maturity at the high school level. Since reading is a form of thinking triggered by printed symbols, it appears essential that our teaching should take cognizance of the stages of logical development and incorporate these, where possible, into our plans for teaching and learning.

References

1. Gray, William S. *Reading in the High School and College.* Forty-Seventh Yearbook of the National Society for the Study of Education, Part II. Chicago: University of Chicago Press, 1948.
2. Jenkinson, Marion D. "Translating the Research in the Structure of Language and Cognition to the Teaching of Reading." *Proceedings of the Conference on Elementary Education, University of Alberta.* Toronto: Holt, Rinehart and Winston (in press).
3. McCallister, James M. "Understanding Paragraph Clues as Aids to Understanding," *Journal of Reading,* Vol. 8, 1964, pp. 11-16.
4. Rawson, Hildred I. *Piaget's Concept of Logical Development and Its Relation to Comprehension in Reading.* Unpublished M. Ed. thesis. University of Alberta, 1965.
5. Russell, David H. *The Dimensions of Children's Meaning Vocabularies in Grades Four Through Twelve.* University of California Series in Education. No. 5. Berkeley: University of California Press, 1954.

GEORGE G. MALLINSON

WESTERN MICHIGAN UNIVERSITY

8. Science Learning and the Problem Reader

A MONG THE VARIOUS subject fields that make up educational programs, there is little doubt that science currently receives more attention than any other. This was not always so. The famous Massachusetts Law of 1642 directed officials of each town to ascertain whether parents and masters were training their charges to read, write and cipher, and in particular "to read and understand the principles of religion and the capital laws of the country." Since the results of placing responsibility on parents and masters proved unsatisfactory, the Massachusetts Law of 1647 was enacted which required that every town of 50 householders or more should appoint a teacher of reading and writing and provide for his wages. Whether such laws were responsible for the direction of academic programs, or whether they merely served as prognosticators is a matter of question. Nevertheless, it is clear that the initial "solids" of the curriculum were English ("reading and writing"), arithmetic ("ciphering"), and history ("laws of the land"), science was notably absent. During the decades that followed, most experiences that might be classified as science were offered mainly for vocational preparation or as part of "classical" or "college-entrance" programs, not for general education. To be sure, some activities related to science, such as nature study, were included in elementary school programs. But, they were not organized sequentially, and were generally "self-contained packages" that bore little relationship to one another.

Many voices were raised from time to time about the inadequacies of such science programs. It was pointed out that science affected everyone and, hence, science programs should be organized for everyone, not just the technician or professional person. However, it was not until 1932, with the publication of Part I of the Thirty-First Yearbook of the National Society for the Study of Education entitled *A Program for*

Teaching Science, that an articulate statement appeared supporting the need for a sequential program of science from the kindergarten to the university. The Yearbook postulated the basic objectives for science education involving both "dimensions of knowledge" and "dimensions of performance," which, although modified in terminology, are much the same as those accepted today. In brief, the Yearbook emphasized that students should "not read about science, but rather should do science." The Yearbook, however, was much less articulate in indicating how the objectives might be implemented in the classroom. In retrospect, one may conclude that science teachers paid homage to what the Yearbook said should happen in the classroom, but there was little impact on the development of activities that fostered intellectual performance. "Doing" objectives in science were generally met by manipulating equipment, expending calories on field trips, and "framing things." Classroom procedures prior to the Yearbook varied little from those after. What was obtained has been aptly described in the statement: "If the students brought in a bird, they stuffed it; if they brought in a rock, they mounted it; if they brought in a leaf, they pressed it! The philosophy was, 'If the thing moved, kill it and nail it to a board.' "

In summary, students read science lessons; wrote answers to science questions; filled out blanks in science workbooks; and slavishly followed directions in what were piously labelled "experiments." It was largely verbal science, and the marriage between science and reading generally seemed to be a happy one.

Science Teaching and Reading

During the period described in the previous section, many investigations involving the relationships between learning science subject-matter and reading factors were undertaken. Some of these studies appear in the list of references in the Appendix. Most of the earlier studies, which were motivated by the general vocabulary studies of Thorndike, Horn, and Buckingham and Dolch, sought mainly to identify the vocabulary deemed to be "essential" or "desirable" for inclusion in science courses at various levels. They were based on the premise that the vocabulary used in a science program is a valid index of the concepts that are dealt with, and also of the level of understanding expected in learning the concepts. The monumental study published in 1938 by Curtis (1), in which the results of over 100 investigations were summarized was probably the high-water mark of these efforts.

About the time of Curtis' major study, the philosophy expressed in the Thirty-First Yearbook concerning the need for science programs for all students began to have impact. The new direction for the programs made it clear that vocabulary load was not the sole criterion of the level of reading or learning difficulty of materials. An even more important criterion of difficulty seemed to be the matrix of non-technical vocabulary and the writing style in which the scientific vocabulary appeared. Among the investigations that were based on this concept were those of Flesch, Dale and Chall, and Lorge. Needless to say, the earlier studies involving vocabulary load, as well as the later ones involving the "gestalt" of the textual material for science were closely heeded by authors and book publishers. Every effort was made to keep the "essential" vocabulary at the appropriate level and to write in a style that enhanced the readability of the material. The vocabulary lists and glossaries provided in science books were used widely, but seldom as wisely as they might have been. Unfortunately, they frequently became the bases of exercises in which science terms and their meanings were memorized.

It should be made clear at this time that many of the science educators who had been deeply involved in vocabulary and reading studies were in the forefront of the movement to "get science teaching out of the book and into the environment." However, the "new" philosophy was not greeted universally with unbridled enthusiasm. Unfortunately, the earlier stereotype of science as a compilation of knowledge generally submerged considerations of the performance dimension. But, even more important, the meaning of "performance" in science was nebulous in the minds of most science teachers and, unfortunately, still is.

During the past ten years, the writer has appeared on many occasions before groups of scientists and science teachers, during which he has used the technique described below to ascertain what they believed to be the purposes of teaching science. Interestingly enough, the reactions to the technique were the same for all teachers, whether they taught at the early elementary level, junior high school level, high school level or university level. As an illustration, one of the audience, a sixth grade teacher, might be selected as a subject. This person was asked to imagine that it was the first full day of school in September and that he was facing his sixth graders on the first full teaching day. He was to remember that they had already had six years of schooling (kindergarten through fifth grade) and they now arrived in his room for further education. He was to assume that he was beginning his program in English, communications, or language arts, whatever name might be appropriate. He was then asked to state what he believed that the students had gained from their previous experiences in English, what they had brought with them, what they had learned, what they'd studied, which would serve as a base for his sixth-grade program. After some deliberation, the responses, "Well, he ought to be able to read," "He ought to be able to write, spell, speak, listen, etc." would be forthcoming. The teacher was then asked to respond to the same query from the previous arithmetic, numbers, or mathematics program. This time there was less hesitation and the teacher would invariably state that the student ought to be able "to add, subtract, multiply, divide, use fractions and decimals, etc." Then the query was directed to science. Usually, there was some hesitation and confusion. However, in practically all cases the first suggestion was that "he ought to know something about either birds (or rocks)." The initial response bred confidence in the teacher and the cohorts who were assisting him with responses, and the list of what "he ought to know" was expanded to include among others planets, weather, trees, and the earth.

The group was then asked to survey the list, which was generally written on a blackboard, to determine whether there was consistency among the statements made for the different subject matter fields. The analysis of the blackboard notes indicated that in English and mathematics, the student was expected to do something better as a result of his experiences whereas in science he was expected to recall the experience he had. To a query as to whether or not science was designed to teach a student to do something better, a hesitating answer was usually, "Well, yes, he ought to think critically and be able to use skills of scientific method." While it would be difficult to disagree with the two objectives, both are clichés and it is doubtful whether any teacher could translate them with a degree of assurance into classroom practice. As of this time, this technique has been used on over 380 occasions and there was no deviation from the results described here.

Thus, it can be seen, for better or for worse, that in the area of science reading subject matter has been heavily emphasized. This discussion is not aimed at arguing the merits of this philosophy, but merely to show that reading has been closely related to the attainment of the objectives of science teaching. The facts indicate that the reading ability of the student, the extent to which the reading difficulty of the science materials was appropriate for the students for whom they were designed, and the emphasis placed on the role of effective reading in learning science were clearly recognized. The extent to which these factors were given cognizance in the classroom is a subject for another paper. Suffice to say, they were considered important.

A Change in Viewpoint

It is interesting to note that despite the emphasis placed on the role of reading in science teaching, reading and vocabulary studies have all but disappeared from the literature of science education since 1955. In fact, some changes in the attitudes expressed recently about science teaching by many scientists and science educators have prompted the writer to publish a paper entitled "Will Books Become Obsolete?" These new attitudes suggest that subject matter can be ignored in the science classroom, particularly at the elementary and junior high school levels, and that the processes of science and laboratory activities should be almost the sole concern.

Prior to 1955, when science education supposedly was the property of teachers' colleges, Departments of Education, and professional educators, the professional educator was roundly castigated in journals and roasted over the fires of righteousness by the scientific community "until the sin dripped out of him like gravy" for his lack of concern with the subject matter content of science courses and his preoccupation with skills and processes. The articles by Fuller, Bestor and many others are ample testimony to his crusade. However, with the advent of the Course Content Improvement Program of the National Science Foundation, the scientific community became involved with the development of science programs of less than college grade and the shoes changed feet.

The statements of philosophy emerging from committees of scientists who worked on these programs are evidence, particularly those statements emerging from the Commission on Science Education of the American Association for the Advancement of Science. These statements suggest that science subject matter is relatively unimportant; sequence may well be ignored in science programs from the kindergarten through the eighth grade; and except for the processes of science and critical thinking there are few other objectives with which science education should be concerned. Obviously, not all scientists hold these viewpoints. However, the educator is now found supporting the role of subject matter.

Several other statements that have been made recently also place some confusion on the place of subject matter in science. On page 58 in the October 15, 1965 issue of *Time* this statement appeared:

At Keppel's suggestion, the Carnegie Corporation is financing the preparation of tests that will measure achievement in reading, language arts, math, social studies, fine arts, vocational education and citizenship. Some tests will be tried out at public schools this winter.

This writer wonders why science was left out. Is it that science subject matter no longer has any validity?

In a testing activity in which the writer was recently engaged, he was surprised to receive some criticism from some scientists about the technical vocabulary that appeared in some items designed for the sixth grade level. Among these terms were *bacteria, insulator, revolution, rotation, orbit, oxidation, digestive, photosynthesis, absorbed, refracted, chlorophyll, stomata, palisade cells, chloroplast,* and *vascular bundles.* Obviously, these words will be difficult for some students if they appear in the text without some form of explanation. Nevertheless, all of them are found in most series of science textbooks from the fourth through sixth grade level. They are, of course, usually explained so that the student is not likely to encounter difficulty. Thus, there seems to be some regression on the part of some scientists for many of them once defended as "rigorous" subject-matter content and the importance of reading skills. This view gives rise to many contradictions, namely, these:

1. The information explosion which has been fostered by the development of digital computers has been publicized extensively, particularly with respect to the sciences. Prior to 1940, it was estimated that scientific knowledge was doubling in volume every fifty years. Thus, the volume of scientific knowledge accumulated between the dawn of history and 1940 would be replicated by 1990. By 1950, the estimated period of doubling had been reduced to ten years. Currently, the period of replication is estimated to be between 5 and 7 years. Although no person could possibly read even a small fraction of the expanding output, the problem of "covering the literature" in one's field of science is hardly being reduced.

2. Several analyses have been made recently of the job activities of scientists. These analyses indicate that, on the average, scientists spend about 14 hours of a 40-hour work week reading materials written by, or writing materials to be read by, persons who are not their occupational peers. They spend an additional 12 hours reading materials written by, or writing materials to be read by, those who are their occupational peers. During the remaining 14 hours, they behave like the stereotypes of scientists. The results of these job

analyses would certainly support the need for communication ability, both in terms of production (writing) and in terms of consumption (reading).

Obviously these contradictions, namely the apparent retreat from subject matter on one hand and the increasing appearance of published materials on the other, demand some resolution. Nearly everyone recognizes that the laboratory must be more than an environment for the expenditure of calories through physical manipulation of hardware and preoccupation with isolated experiences. It must provide opportunity for developing meanings and perceptions of the experiences offered, and these are obtained only through a background of knowledge. A student cannot be expected to learn basic principles without first having the foundational knowledges. A laboratory experience without such knowledges would be tantamount to teaching naval architecture by handing the student a log and a piece of sharpened stone and leaving him on his own. Obviously, students cannot be put through the cultural heritage of all scientific effort. Consequently, the development of meanings and perceptions must rest with their ability to read foundational materials, whether or not these learnings take place at the early elementary level or at the university level. The implications of this statement were well summarized by Smith (2) in the following quotation:

> Words are an important part of the culture of a people. But words are far more than mere symbols to be used in communication. They are also tools for thinking. For higher-level thinking, words act as shorthand in that certain words contain the distilled essence of numerous experiences. Thus, though we often hear it said that a picture can replace a thousand words, it may be important that certain of our words stand for a thousand of life's pictures.

It is postulated, therefore, that without regard for the level at which science experiences are offered, reading will still be one of the major means of input for the student. It is postulated, also, that unless the student has accumulated a certain amount of subject matter through reading to serve as a background for his learning, his science learning is almost sure to be randomized and minimal. This will be particularly true for the student who is the problem reader at the secondary-level. These students are subject to the information explosion as much as the more able student. Their likelihood of becoming scientifically literate and serving as knowledgeable laymen in a scientific environment will depend largely on their ability to absorb some elements of scientific information rapidly and efficiently through reading. They are not the people who will work in the laboratory or carry out investigations, thus gaining scientific knowledge. Rather, these knowledges will come largely through what they read both in school and as adults in published materials. But, before the problems of the problem reader in high school can be solved, particularly with reference to science, a number of questions must be faced. Among them are: "What is a problem reader?" "Is the problem reader a poor reader of all materials?" "What materials are most suitable for the problem reader?" "What techniques may work best with the problem reader?"

Working With the Problem Reader in the High School Classroom

Any effort to describe the problem reader precisely would require far more space than is available for the entire report and, hence, it will not be attempted. However, for the purpose of this presentation, the problem reader will be considered to be a student in grades seven through twelve who does not read fluently enough to attain minimally-acceptable standards of understanding of those textual materials in science designed for students at his grade level. However, the presentation will be confined to students whose deficiencies are related primarily to "inadequate organization" of the impulses that reach the brain on the optic nerve, or those whose difficulties are motivational in origin. It will not include those with physical defects that need medical attention. Together, these two groups make up most of those considered to be "problem readers" at the high school level.

The problem reader in science is most likely to be found in the ninth and tenth grade science courses, since these persons are likely to be discouraged from taking the more specialized science courses in the eleventh and twelfth grades, usually chemistry and physics. They may take a terminal general physical science course in the senior year, although this is not typical. Thus, such students who elect science are likely to find themselves in *general* science, *general* biology, or *general* physical science. Their attendance in such courses increases the difficulties facing them as problem readers. Among these difficulties are the following:

1. The contents of the general courses in the sciences are taken from many science disciplines rather than one. Hence, the basic vocabularies of such courses are likely to be more extensive than those of the specialized courses. Also, the terms in the vocabulary are likely to be used less frequently than those of the specialized courses.

2. In the previous sections, the current emphasis in many quarters on laboratory activity, with a commensurate reduction of emphasis on subject matter content has been described. However, this new philosophy, without regard for its merit, has had little impact on the general courses in science. These courses are still highly verbal, laboratory activities being minimal and generally consisting of teacher demonstrations. Thus, the problem reader is likely to be faced with more reading than his peers in specialized courses who read more ably.

3. The general courses are more likely to be staffed with inexperienced teachers than are the specialized courses. Contrary to pious protestations, the general courses require teachers with more extensive science backgrounds than the specialized courses, if they are to be taught effectively. For this reason, as well as others, the general courses in science are more difficult to teach than the specialized courses. However, in deference to seniority, science teachers with greater experience are assigned to the specialized courses where their more extensive "accumulations of wisdom" are allegedly needed.

4. Few teachers at the high school level have been trained in the techniques involved in the teaching of reading, or the principles involved in learning to read. Unfortunately, reading instruction in the high school science classroom frequently consists of distributing dittoed or mimeographed lists of "essential terms," together with their definitions. In some cases, students may be expected to supply definitions whose accuracies are frequently open to question. The student then memorizes the terms and the definitions (possibly *ersatz*). Attainment of a criterion score is evidence *ipso facto* that the reading problem is eliminated.

In addition to all these "positive" factors working "for" the problem reader, it is generally conceded that scientific vocabulary is growing about three times as rapidly as that in any other field. In addition, the connotations of scientific terms are changing rapidly.

With all these considerations it is possible to make several questionable moves:

1. Let the student remain a problem reader and "fish for himself." With such a philosophy, the teacher may emulate the action of the social worker who was attempting to persuade an individual to receive aid from the "anti-poverty program." The potential recipi-

ent stood on his right as an American citizen to be poor and dirty. Faced with such logic, the social worker retreated. One must assume, however, that the problem reader in the high school classroom does not have an analogous privilege and that any resistance must be circumvented.

2. Completely and permanently discard all accepted procedures for working with problem readers on the philosophy that "if you can't raise the bridge, lower the river." Students on leaving high school, whether before or after graduation, are expected to read standard materials and their scientific environments will still demand their adjustments.

Then, what positive actions can and should be taken? The answers to this question are not simple or categoric, and their implementation requires effort. The problems involved in the implementation will not be discussed here, but problems should not be regarded as roadblocks, rather only temporary barriers to be circumvented.

1. *Time must be taken to assist the problem reader in the high school classroom.* Anyone with young children has no doubt been annoyed by their "undesirable activities" when adult members wanted to relax and enjoy television. The comment typical of parents, "Go on upstairs, get a toy and play with it and behave yourself," has been the subject of intensive research investigation and has been found to be ineffective—significant at the 1 per cent level. A similar finding, also significant at the 1 per cent level, holds true for the comment commonly made to the problem reader, "You'll find some books and magazines on the subject on the table in the back of the room. Go read them!"

The writer does not believe it is within the scope of this paper to discuss the source of the necessary time, but success depends on the expenditure of extra time.

2. *Explain the textbook.* The writer hastens to state immediately that he does not believe that the memorization of a textbook represents the accomplishment of a science course. *He does not believe this at all!* However, he assumes that the common practice of using a basal textbook will be followed and that the problem reader will have one. Thus, it should be used in the optimal fashion.

A study now underway by the writer concerns the ways in which teachers of high school science use textbooks. The technique for gathering information is somewhat arduous, involving indirect interviews, since a questionnaire which would elicit responses rapidly, would most likely elicit responses with dubious validity. Data, collected so far from more than ninety high school science teachers in ten widely-distributed states, indicate that fewer than 5 per cent explain the various features of the textbook in use and allegedly designed to aid the student. These features include the typical introduction to the student; the glossary and index; and suggestions for using the textbook that may appear in the teacher's manual or teacher's edition.

It is certainly reasonable to suggest that the problem reader will benefit greatly from time spent by the teacher in explaining these features. The student should be expected to select terms from the glossary and locate them in the text. He should become familiar with the roles of footnotes and captions. Phonetic spellings of technical terms should be studied and their significance in understanding the textual material clarified.

The students may well be asked to prepare outlines of several chapters by copying the headings and subheadings and placing them in the appropriate hierarchies. The teacher may reproduce two short subsections of text material minus the subheadings and have the students identify the subheadings in the outlines they have prepared under which the text materials belong. They may be asked to determine whether the information in one or more captions for illustrations duplicates information in the text, even if phrased somewhat differently; whether it extends or amplifies information in the text, or whether it is entirely different. With any of these procedures, the student should be expected to give the reasons for his responses. The writer is not so naïve as to assume that these techniques, or for that matter any other teaching technique, will evoke lavish praise from the problem reader or any other student. However, familiarity with the textbook is likely to hasten more salutary learning than the lack of familiarity.

3. *The use of materials other than the basal textbook should be planned carefully.* This statement might seem to be the epitome of the self-evident and probably is. But, classroom action does not always fit the philosophy expressed. At this point, the writer wishes to express some concern about the use of textbooks designed for lower grades or multiple "peer textbooks" to provide for the problem reader. Textbooks for earlier grades which may not be too difficult for the problem reader are invariably below the level of his social sophistication and certainly can be a stimulus to his disdain. "Peer" or competing textbooks, while they may differ somewhat in approach, on the average, are not likely to be greatly different from the basal textbook in content. A problem reader has

generally been so designated because of his problems with standard materials such as textbooks, and hence analogous materials are not likely to offer much of a solution.

Many materials with the appropriate levels of sophistication, but with lower levels of reading difficulty are available, including some issues of *Science World;* articles in *Life* and other magazines; and some newspaper articles. Such items may be supplied for the problem reader if they are appropriate in topic and reading level. The problem reader may be asked to read them and then read his textbook carefully. He should attempt to identify and list key ideas found in both the supplementary material and his textbook. He should then do the same for key ideas found *only* in his textbook. In this way, his reading effort required for discrimination rather than only absorption and his application to the task may be enhanced. This technique may well be suitable for the problem reader plagued with low ability, as well as for the one lacking motivation.

4. *Compare the usage of terms.* In advertisements, scientific terms are frequently used in the way that seems most expedient. A technique that may take advantage of that expediency may be useful with the problem reader. He may be assigned the task of listing scientific terms that appear in advertisements, magazines, and newspapers, together with the meanings assigned to them, and the contexts in which they appear. Such words may include *power, energy, force, work, germ,* and *food,* as well as others. The next task is to read the textbook or other materials available in the classroom and compare the *scientific* meanings of the terms with those assigned to them in what are hopefully "authoritative" reading materials. The meanings in the two different sources should then be compared for likenesses and differences, as well as for inaccuracies that may be evident. Obviously, the textbook will need to be read in order for comparisons to be made. However, the students' efforts with the less demanding material in the advertisements may serve as a springboard for an attack on the standard materials that are likely to prove more difficult.

5. *Make use of "science corners" in newspapers.* During the past few years, there have appeared in many newspapers syndicated columns such as "Kousin Klod's Science Korner." The qualifications for Kousin Klod seem to be residence in an institution for the mentally deficient, a dropout at the kindergarten level, or an undergraduate major in mythology. This writer has yet to see one column that has been free from error. Most of the columns seem to be designed for the upper elementary or junior high school levels, and hence are appropriate as motivational material to work

with problem readers in the high school classroom. The teacher may well survey the newspapers and classify the answers to various questions that are submitted according to topic (this, incidently, seems to be the general format). The students may be handed the questions and answers related to the appropriate topics and asked to read their textbooks and other materials in the classroom to determine what errors may be propagated by Kousin Klod. One preliminary activity, of course, will be the location of the errors by the teacher. Again, the student will move from less difficult material and the activity described should provide some motivation for the student to read and reasonably improve his reading ability.

6. *Develop reading through activities involving inquiry and the processes of science.* Activities recommended for developing inquiry and processes of science frequently fail to meet acceptable criteria. They often require slavish adherence to directions and duplication of manipulations that could be accomplished by a chimpanzee, if he could be kept in one place long enough. Without further regard for this point, however, the pursuit of inquiry skills may well be adapted to the problem reader with a view toward his reading ability as well as his skills of inquiry. As one example, the student may be asked to perform one of the activities and formulate the conclusions that may emerge. He may then be asked to read ancillary literature available in the classroom or in the library at home and develop from his gleanings another activity which might be directed toward the same purposes. This may be written up as an exercise similar to the one which he was expected to perform oirginally. There are, of course, many different ways in which this technique could be modified, but space limitations prevent their being mentioned here.

Summary

The suggestions that have been made for working with the problem reader in the high school science classroom are based on a number of assumptions that are described earlier. The writer believes that the assumptions are amply supported by research evidence from numerous sources. The suggestions made here are, of course, designed for the use of the teacher, not for direct transmittal to the student. They must be used along with the appropriate topics and the successful pedagogies that have proved to be operationally efficient. Not all of them may work in one situation. In many situations, none may work without adaptation, and that is to be expected.

The teacher should not assume that the techniques will be panaceas for problem readers because they probably will not be. But, judiciously used, they may be sufficient to raise the reading ability of the problem reader in science to a level of minimal acceptability.

REFERENCES

1. Curtis, Francis D. *Investigations of Vocabulary in Textbooks of Science for Secondary Schools.* Boston: Ginn and Compnay, 1938.
2. Smith, Henry P ."The Perpetual Determinants of Effective Reading With Some Social Implications." *The University of Kansas Bulletin of Education,* XIX, Spring Issue, May 1965, 82-83.

RICHARD H. MUELDER

UNIVERSITY OF CHICAGO LABORATORY SCHOOLS

9. Helping Students Read Mathematics

THERE ARE really two objectives involved in helping a student improve in the reading of mathematics. From the math teacher's point of view, the most important objective is to help his students learn mathematics. But the teacher realizes that the improvement of reading skills is important in his teaching. Reading is a skill which every teacher in all subject areas should strive to teach.

This chapter is based primarily on the writer's experiences in dealing with high school mathematics students. The suggestions and techniques to be described have resulted from talks with many people: math teachers, reading consultants, and others. The suggestions are not supported by objective research, but they have worked in mathematics classes, to some degree at least.

Readiness

A math teacher can do a number of things before he even meets his classes. One of the first should be to collect useful test results and then to interpret these results with regard to their implications for the coming year. There are three things this action accomplishes. In the first place, the test results can help to define the limits of the problem. In my own school, for example, the sophomore class has a seven year range in reading ability. More specifically, there are members of the present sophomore class who are reading at the sixth grade level and others who are reading at the college freshman level. The mathematics teacher, as teachers in other areas, faces a wide range of reading ability. This range is, of course, reflected not only in reading scores but in aptitude scores, achievement scores, and so on. (In trying to realize the implications of this wide range, I try to put myself in the position of the students at these various levels. I try to imagine how the sixth grade student would react to being faced

102

with a high school sophomore's textbook. On the other hand, it is unlikely that a college freshman would be challenged by a high school sophomore's textbook.)

I first look at the test results as a way to define my problem. If a school does tracking in mathematics (i.e., makes some attempt at homogeneous grouping for math instruction) then one of the things to be considered in organizing the groups in addition to ability and achievement in mathematics is the reading scores. This will be of great assistance in placing a student into his correct group.

Secondly, test scores can also suggest categories of problems. For example, it may be that students who have high reading speed scores but lower comprehension scores may need help in adjusting to the reading situation in math. If a student, on the other hand, has reading scores which are fairly consistent (i.e., both reading speed and reading comprehension are either very low or high) then this indicates another sort of problem. Therefore, an analysis of the reading scores can help in pinpointing the types of problems the math teacher faces.

Thirdly, the reading test scores can spotlight individual students who may have problems in a math course, problems which are at least partly based on the student's reading difficulties. In addition to comprehension and speed scores, the vocabulary scores can be used to indicate students whose deficiency in general vocabulary may block their comprehension in expository mathematics reading. By identifying these students, the math teacher can take appropriate steps to help the student.

Prior to meeting his classes the mathematics teacher should choose materials carefully. If the teacher is going to have a heterogeneous class, then it is probably best to select a text whose reading difficulty matches the reading average for the class. On the other hand, if the classes are going to be homogeneously grouped, then the math teacher and his colleagues in the mathematics department ought to consider the possibility of choosing different textbooks for the different groups. In order to do this, the math teacher and his colleagues must be as familiar as possible with the various math textbooks and be able to make judgments about levels of reading difficulty.

Another area to which the mathematics teacher needs to give attention before meeting with his classes is the selection of supplementary reading materials. If materials other than a single textbook are to be used, the same criteria should be followed as in the selection of the math textbook. However, here the teacher has an opportunity to provide materials at a variety of levels of difficulty which will allow each student to work at his own level.

In teaching a class where there is a predominance of poor readers, the math teacher should deal realistically with the problem of teaching these students mathematics through judicious selection of audio-visual aids and easier reading materials. As a matter of fact, giving "background" help of this nature may help a student to read materials which would otherwise be too difficult for him. When dealing with the question of how to help students read mathematics, one should always bear in mind that one's primary responsibility as a mathematics teacher is to teach mathematics. Though helping the student to read mathematics is an important factor in this area, it is only one of the factors. Even with help from a special reading teacher, the math teacher cannot overnight bring the ability of a poor reader up to an acceptable level. It may be necessary for the math teacher to find other ways of getting his material across. That is, when a math teacher gives a reading assignment, he should always have in mind that there will be a certain number of students to whom he will have to give more individual attention. Unless this is done, there is a strong likelihood that they will not get from their reading assignments what is expected of them. In general, when the math teacher familiarizes himself with the materials to be used, he must anticipate any reading problems that might be involved.

It is possible that the math teacher may not know how to go about using the techniques mentioned above. He may not know the best ways to evaluate test results; he may not know how to go about evaluating levels of reading difficulty in various materials; and he may not know what other aids are available to him. It is at this point that the reading consultant, if the school system has one, can be of great help. From my own personal experience I know that Miss Ellen Thomas, Reading Consultant at the Laboratory Schools, has been of invaluable assistance to me and other teachers in this regard.

Specific Activities

The following discussion indicates the things that I tried to do during the school year to help my students become better readers of mathematical material. The first thing that is of help to students is to make it clear that one of the objectives in math education is the improvement of reading ability in mathematics. I try to be as honest with them as possible about the problems that they face in this area. As early in the year as is feasible

I give them an assignment which is entirely devoted to reading and involves no written work. I do this because I think it emphasizes for them the importance of becoming good readers of mathematics. In making this assignment I spend fifteen to twenty-five minutes discussing reading procedures necessary to the successful completion of the assignment. In this discussion I indicate to them how they can improve their reading.

I emphasize several areas. First, I feel very strongly that the problem of adjusting speed for mathematics reading is of really crucial importance. Therefore, I try to stress the importance of this. Secondly, I am very concerned with the problem of vocabulary building. Lastly, I want to emphasize that since the topic selected is one with which the students are not familiar, it is important not to rely upon this reading to take care of all the learning for all of the students. I make a point to see those students who are likely to have had trouble with the reading and to give them individual instruction on the specific topic.

The following is an edited transcription from a tape recording of part of one of my classes. Student questions and responses are not included.

Your next assignment is going to be entirely a reading assignment. Would you look at it with me for a moment on page 63 in your textbook. Your assignment for tomorrow—Friday—is to read section 3-4 on convex sets. Now that's going to be the only new assignment—just that reading. I'm not going to ask you to do any more problems. I'm doing this for a purpose. I want to take this opportunity to talk with you about ways you can use your textbook more effectively than I think you are using it. I think some of you are going to be disappointed when you see your test grades, and think that one of the ways I can help you do better (which is what I'm here for)' is to give you some suggestions about methods to use your textbook more effectively. So I want to take the time today to talk with you about doing reading assignments in mathematics.

This is the first assignment in which you're going to be on your own. It's a new topic. Some of you may have some vague notions about convex sets, but I am sure that most of you have never heard of the idea before, so it's going to be a new idea to dig out on your own. And, therefore, you've got to be prepared to spend time on it. It's only three pages, but three pages of math reading is probably equivalent to forty or fifty pages of a novel and perhaps equivalent to twenty or thirty pages of a social studies assignment. Just because a math assignment consists of a few pages doesn't mean that it's the kind of thing about which you can say, "Oh boy, he only gave us three pages to read for tomorrow. I can do that in five minutes and then watch TV." Now it's possible to do that. You can "read" this in five minutes or less, no question about it. But you won't be doing your assignment. All you'd be doing would be reading a bunch of words. And you won't be coming up with the vital information you should be getting out of this assignment. So let's talk about that for a few minutes.

First, I've said that mathematics reading is different from reading in other subjects. Maybe you'll understand this statement a little better if you understand why. It's because mathematical writing is different. The people who write mathematics write in a different style than people who write in other subjects. It's not that one fellow is wrong and the other fellow is right; it's just a difference among subjects.

Mathematical reading is more densely packed than other reading. By that I mean there are more ideas per square inch, per page, per sentence in math reading than there are in a novel or short story. In math reading, every single word is crucial. A single word may change the whole meaning of a sentence or a phrase. So there's one important thing to remember—it's highly packed with ideas.

Also, it's at a different level of abstraction than most of the reading involved in novels, for instance. In a novel you are reading descriptions of what people are doing and what people look like and what they say to each other and what scenes are like—concrete things that you're used to every day. But mathematics is at a high level of abstraction; therefore, it's more difficult to read.

So how should you go about reading a math assignment? Let's take a little time to talk about your approach to tomorrow's assignment. First adjust your speed. Have several speeds. Just as a car has several gears to go at different speeds for different purposes, so you have to have gears that you can shift as far as your reading is concerned. So begin by shifting down to a moderate speed and read through the assignment once without any stops. If somewhere on the second page there's a sentence or a paragraph that you don't quite understand, don't stop! Go on. You're going to come back, so go on. Read through it once at a moderate speed. Now what's the purpose of this? It will give you a sort of general idea, a general feeling of what it's all about, of what the author is trying to do.

You all know the story, I'm sure, of the blind men and the elephant. Each one felt a different part of the elephant and one fellow said it was a tree because he felt the legs, and another said it was a snake because he felt the trunk. Each of them had a different impression of what the elephant was like because he was sensing or feeling a different part of the animal. Well, now you may be in the same spot. You may not understand a part of this reading if you just look at the part itself, but if you've read through the whole thing and have a general view of it, then you may get a better idea of what's going on. Therefore, the paragraph or sentence you did not understand on the second page may become clear when you have read all three pages. So that's the first thing to do. Read through the assignment once at a moderate speed and then go back and reread.

Now, I can't follow you home. You're going to do what you want to do. But I do not believe that there's anybody, no matter how good a reader he is, who can read through a math assignment without rereading it once. It just can't be done except in very unusual cases. By the way, fast readers are sometimes the ones who have the most trouble with reading mathematics because they're so used to whizzing through their ordinary reading that they are just unable to slow up unless they make a serious effort.

Okay, now you're going back and reread, and I want to talk to you about how that rereading should be done. The second time through, get out pencil and paper and read with pencil and paper. What do I mean by that? I mean that you've got to be prepared to stop and use pencil and paper to help you understand the basic information in the reading. Let me give you an example of that right here. Suppose you're reading a passage of algebra and the author uses the equation $8x - 7 = 4x + 13$. Then in the very next sentence he says, "Therefore $x = -5$." Now is there anyone in here who can look at that and, boom, tell that's a correct result? I couldn't. Well, *is* that right? No, it's *positive* 5, isn't it? You can't tell just by looking at it. If you took the author's word for it and said, "Okay, I'll go on; I just won't pay attention to it," then there are two dangers involved.

One danger is that sometimes authors make mistakes. We caught one just yesterday in the exercises. Remember the picture that wasn't drawn right? Okay. Books are misprinted, and what in the world is the sense in your reading a whole assignment in mathematics and not knowing what's going on simply because the printer made a little mistake? Everyone makes mistakes. So that's one possibility.

The second danger is poor comprehension. If you stop and take the few seconds or the minute necessary to work out the intervening steps, then you will understand better what's going on. So, when I say read with pencil and paper, I mean for the purpose of stopping to work out inner steps that the author has left out. You'll discover that the farther you get in mathematics, the more the author is going to rely on your ability to fill in the elementary steps between. So you've got to be ready to stop and work them out if you're really going to understand.

There is another thing, and this, I think, is best illustrated by taking a look at the beginning of your assignment for Friday. Notice how it starts. It begins by talking about convex sets, and the authors have drawn some pictures for you. First they have drawn pictures of things that are supposed to be convex sets and then pictures of things that are supposed to be non-convex sets. You should supplement that with your own examples. After you've read this and you think you understand what a convex set is, draw another picture while you're reading. Do it on a piece of scratch paper at the side of your book. If you understand what a convex set is, you ought to be able to draw a good example of it. Draw an example of something you think is not a convex set. Compare your examples with the book's and with the definition given. Make sure that you understand before you go on.

Another thing—I don't think there's anything like it in this particular reading assignment, but you'll run across assignments in which the authors will give a definition without accompanying pictures. But that doesn't mean that you shouldn't stop and make your own illustration. For one thing, if it's really good definition, if the authors have really given you a good explanation, their description should be clear enough so that you could draw a picture based on their description. So, when they're describing a parallelogram, you ought to be able, from their word description, to draw a picture. If you can read the definition and then illustrate it, the chances of your really understanding what's going on are much better. So be prepared to draw pictures and draw figures of the definitions and explanations in your reading.

As you read through the assignment, be prepared to ask questions of the author. Because it's in print doesn't mean that it's the truth forever and ever. Be critical. Ask why. If you read a sentence, ask, "How does he have a right to say that?" "Why is that true?" "How can he justify saying that?" Ask yourself such questions. There are two reasons for doing this. If you ask yourself the questions, and then satisfy yourself in your own mind that the author has supplied the vital information, then you really understand what's going on. If you just read it over and say, "Okay, I'll accept that," without any question, then you may forget about it. But if you've questioned it and convinced yourself that it's right, then you're more likely to remember it.

There is another reason for asking yourself these questions. By next March or April, you will be writing some mathematics of your own. And one of the things you're going to have to get used to is to critically analyze the things you say. You've got to be prepared to ask yourself, "Why do I think that's true?" "Why does that make sense to me?" "How could I explain it to the person sitting next to me?" If you've gotten into the habit of asking questions in your reading assignments, and of being able to find the answers, then you've started to develop a habit that will help you ask those questions of yourselves.

One of the problems that some students have in mathematics is that they are overwhelmed with the amount of new vocabulary they must acquire.

So how can you work on this problem of vocabulary? There are several ways. You remember when we first started talking about your math notebook, I mentioned that I was going to ask you to maintain a glossary of the new words you ran across. Now, I'm going to ask you to start a glossary of the new words with definitions, as we come across them.

If you really want this to pay off, keep it up to date, day by day. Take two minutes—that's about all it will take—to enter each of the new terms that we get into your glossary. Now, what's the purpose of this? Well, it helps comprehension and retention. If you hear me say a word and get it through your ears, and you read it in your textbook and you get it through your eyes, and then you get your writing muscles involved in the learning process, believe it or not, all these approaches help you remember. Your glossary can help you also as you review for tests, for example. Organize it by units, and at the end of a unit, draw a double line. Then if you want to go back and look at the new words you've had in a unit, you know where to find them.

Come January, when we're well into this book, you may be reading an assignment and come across a word that you're not too sure of. The best example I can give of this is the word "between." Every one of you thought you knew what that word meant before you walked into this room in September. But I bet that none of you knew what the mathematical definition of it was. So what's going to happen next January when you see the word "between" and say, "Sure, I know what that means." Unconsciously you may accept the word and go on, and then a couple of sentences later the author is doing something you don't understand. You'll look up in disgust and say, "I don't understand what's going on." You know what the trouble may be? You may be using the everyday meaning of "between," forgetting for the moment the mathematical definition. And it may be that what the author is doing two sentences later depends on your knowing what the mathematical definition of "between" is. Therefore, another use of your glossary is to have it available so that if you need to look up a word, you know immediately where to find it.

One more comment about vocabulary. In addition to using your glossaries in the ways indicated, be prepared to use words in different ways than you use them in other classes. Get into the habit of accuracy and precision in your math class. One of the things that makes poetry beautiful and worth while is that words can have different meanings. When someone writes a poem describing a battlefield in the First World War, there can be many interpretations of what the poet saw and what his special language means. Various people will get various meanings out of a poem. This ambiguity is a good thing in poetry. But that very thing would be catastrophic in mathematics. It doesn't mean that poetry is bad, nor does it mean that mathematics is bad. It means they're different things. In mathematics, precision is absolutely necessary, while in a poem, being able to accept a wide variety of meanings is absolutely necessary. So be prepared to shift gears between classes.

Follow-up

If a discussion such as the preceding is to be effective, there must be immediate follow-up. Therefore, at the next meeting of the class, I give a short quiz covering the reading assignment. I do this before there is any further classroom work on the topic concerned. There are two reasons for this. First, it gives me an idea of just how effective the discussion of reading a math assignment has been. (I must add that the results have convinced me of the fact that a one-shot effort in this area is not enough.)

Secondly, I think it emphasizes in the students' minds the fact that their mathematics teacher feels that this is something that they need to work on. This is particularly true for the fast reader who may be overconfident about his reading ability—the student who doesn't really believe that he needs to re-read a mathematics assignment. Quite often the shallowness of their reading will be revealed to these students when they discover in taking the quiz that they do not know all that is expected of them.

Using this lesson as a reference, I frequently make comments about the reading skills necessary in mathematics. Too often a math teacher will say to a class, "Do the problems on page such and such," and devote his efforts to discussing how they should go about doing the problems. He may as an afterthought, say, "By the way, read the two or three pages in your textbook preceding these problems," making no further comment about the reading. This is not enough.

It is important that the teacher make clear to his students that they ask questions while reading the assignment; but for most students it will be necessary to help them do this. Therefore, in preparing an assignment in mathematics which involves reading, the teacher ought to discuss briefly some questions they should have in mind in doing their reading. Students should be reminded that the reading assignment is as important as the exercises, and that they should give it more than just cursory attention.

This involves, of course, some preparation on the teacher's part. He must give some thought to the areas that might cause reading trouble and prepare appropriate questions and comments that will help the students over these difficulties.

Another thing that ought to be done sometime before the middle of the year is to have a lesson which follows up the previous discussion on how to read a math assignment. An appropriate opportunity should be chosen when it is obvious to the teacher *and* to the students that they have not successfully completed a reading assignment in mathematics. The teacher can demonstrate the correct procedures forcing the class as much as possible to follow the techniques that will be helpful for them.

Begin by having the class read through the assignment once at a moderate speed. Then lead a brief discussion of what the major ideas involved in the assignment are. It is important in this preliminary discussion not to let the class go too much into detail—emphasizing for them the fact that this first reading was simply designed to give a broad picture of what was going on. Then have individual members of the class read portions of the assignment aloud in turn, making them go slowly. Interrupt them at crucial parts; when they should stop and draw a picture, when some figuring should be done, or when another example should be found. Encourage other members of the class to interrupt the reader when there is something they don't understand clearly. Interrupt the reader and let other students do so when it seems appropriate to ask a question or when it seems a good idea to check on a technical word.

When the class is finished with this slow re-reading have them all re-read a second time at a moderate pace. Finally, have them close their books and take a quiz on the material covered by the reading. The answers to the quiz are given immediately afterward. Most of the time the students are very pleased to discover how well they have done. Point out to them their success on this quiz as compared to the less successful quiz results on other readings, suggesting that perhaps the improved score was the result of having read their assignment more carefully, more thoroughly, and more intelligently than they had done before.

Another reading problem the math teacher faces is improving his students' ability to solve so-called word problems. This is a perennial problem for which I have no absolute solution. However, it is certainly a very important part of a student's math education. It goes to the heart of the student's ability to apply mathematical training to situations outside the math classroom. This, of course, is a central objective in studying mathematics.

One of the critical things for the math teacher to find out when dealing with a word problem that his students have not been able to solve is whether or not the trouble is the result of failure to understand the mathematics involved or failure to have comprehended the reading. These are, of course, closely related, but I think they can be at times differentiated. One method that I have used with some success in helping my students and myself to make this differentiation is as follows. I ask a student to tell me from memory (with his book closed) exactly what the problem is and what data are given with which he is to find the solution. Usually the student will not be able to do this. I then point out to the class that, if they are to successfully solve a word problem, they must have read the problem well enough in order to have at their immediate command all the data available. This means they must have read the problem thoroughly enough to be able to know the principal factors without having to look at the book. I have the class read and re-read the problem until they are able to do this. I have found that after the students are able to state the problem from memory, and in their own words, that some members of the class are then able to solve the problem.

When a student comes to me for extra help with a word problem, I have the student read the problem aloud. I encourage him to read aloud any word problems he faces. I think that the major emphasis given to silent reading makes some students think that it is somehow wrong ever to read aloud to oneself. This is not true in doing a word problem. I point out to the student that one should bring to bear all of the available senses, including hearing. The student who is having trouble with a word problem because he is a poor reader may be able to solve the problem if he hears it.

When working on word problems, all students should be encouraged to draw pictures of the situation involved. If a figure is appropriate, they should be encouraged to label it and to study the relationships involved among its various parts. Another procedure that often works is to have the students make a guess as to what the answer is. It is not important that this guess be accurate. What is important is that the student test his guess with the data given and in so doing, see how the data given are related to the answer wanted. After having done this, students very often can set up a problem using a variable, replacing the previous guess with the variable. They can then proceed to solve the problem.

In any contact with the students for extra help purposes, the math teacher should bear in mind possible reading problems that particular students may have. He should be prepared to give advice and help to such students in improving their reading ability. For example, a student who seems to be having trouble mastering all the additional vocabulary demanded by his math course might be advised to make flash cards. The technical word and an accompanying figure can be on one side with the precise definition and other comments on the back. The student should be urged to use these cards as a study device.

Another way in which students can be helped to master the vocabulary of mathematics is to point out Greek or Latin roots and to assist them in learning to pronounce new words correctly. A student has not incorporated a word into his vocabulary until he can pronounce it properly. Therefore, when a new word is introduced, I repeat it as often as I can, trying for a few days to avoid using pronouns that stand for that word. I try to get the students to use these words in class discussion as frequently as possible.

If the math teacher encounters a student with serious reading difficulties, it may be that a referral to a special reading teacher is called for. The math teacher should, of course, consult with the special reading teacher and discuss with that teacher the student's problems as the math teacher sees them. In cases where special reading instruction is not possible, a reading teacher may be able to suggest ways in which the math teacher can help the student.

Concluding Statement

Most of the remarks I have made apply primarily to the poorer readers in the math class. But we should not forget our responsibility to the better readers in providing them with opportunities to grow. To do this, I recommend books in our library which will be a real challenge to the better readers. I encourage these students to read these books, urging that they attack them in the same way that they attack their math textbook. I give these students opportunities to report to the class the results of their reading. I have found that this is beneficial both for the student doing the extra reading and for the rest of the class as well. It provides a change of pace from the usual classroom routine. If one of the poorer readers asks to do extra reading, I must be prepared to recommend something at his reading level.

I hope that efforts will be continued, involving both secondary school teachers in the various subject areas and reading specialists, to find ways in which the subject matter teacher can help his students become more effective readers. I believe that my efforts in this area have made me a better mathematics teacher.

NILA BANTON SMITH
GLASSBORO STATE COLLEGE

10. Questions Administrators Ask About Reading in Secondary Schools

A T THE PRESENT time administrators in secondary schools are asking many questions about reading. In general, these people have majored in administration and naturally they have not specialized in reading instruction. Furthermore, it is only recently, as educational history goes, that the teaching of reading has been considered an appropriate subject for secondary students. Currently, however, high school administrators are becoming keenly interested in reading. They are eager to do something worthwhile in reading in their respective schools, and they are actively seeking information and advice. This is a built-in opportunity for specialists in reading to be of service to those who are so largely responsible for school policies.

This chapter presents and discusses some of the questions that secondary school administrators are asking about corrective reading and related aspects of reading instruction. The questions are bona fide. They have been asked of the writer while working with superintendents and principals in various localities, and, interestingly enough, the same questions have been asked repeatedly in different parts of the country. So it would appear that these questions are fairly representative of the concerns of many secondary school administrators.

Will You Define Terms Used to Designate Different Kinds of Reading Instruction?

When a teacher tells his administrator that the International Reading Association has a new monograph on *Corrective Reading,* the latter, if he responds true to form, will ask, "Just what is corrective reading?"

The above prediction is based on a very common reaction which comes from administrators when a reading specialist gives a talk to them: "You

114

reading people use so many different terms. You talk about remedial reading, corrective reading, developmental reading and power reading. This is all very confusing. How do these kinds of reading differ?"

Without a doubt these terms are confusing to a person who does not specialize in the field. In fact, reading authorities themselves are not agreed on exactly the same definition for each of these different terms. While fine distinctions may be made, the terms are generally useful in designating different kinds of reading instruction provided for different purposes to students with different degrees of difficulty or competence.

Perhaps a brief story of the evolution of terms, used to differentiate various kinds of reading instruction, will help to clarify this situation. Specialized work with children who were having difficulty in reading was first undertaken by men in the medical profession and by psychologists during the decades between 1880 and 1910 (4). The work of these professional people was done in laboratories. The terms they used to identify the difficulties of their cases were "reading inferiority," "reading disability," or "reading deficiency."

Between 1910 and 1920, reading tests came into use and the results revealed that thousands of children in the public schools were not reading as well as they should. So school administrators and teachers became concerned. They began providing instruction for these retarded readers and they called this instruction *remedial reading*. The writer's research (4) reveals that the first use of the term *remedial reading* in the literature of reading, appeared in an article by Willis Uhl (5) in a periodical published in 1916. Anderson and Merton (1) used the term in an article published in 1920 and Gray (3) used it in a monograph which appeared in 1922. During the initial use of the term, and for many years afterwards, *remedial reading* designated the kind of instruction given to groups of retarded readers in schools.

In the years that elapsed between 1916 and 1940, only two kinds of reading were ever distinguished from one another. These were *reading* and *remedial reading*. During this period, remedial reading was extended into the secondary school, and it became quite common to provide retarded readers at this level with special instruction.

It was in 1941 that the new term *developmental reading* came into our midst. This term was introduced by Bond and Bond. It was used to designate the difference between remedial reading in secondary schools and reading instruction given to those who didn't need special help but for whom continued growth was desirable. The Bonds (2) explain developmental reading as follows:

> The secondary school developmental reading program is concerned fundamentally with the continued refinement and development of the more mature aspects of the self-same types of abilities that were being refined and developed in the elementary school. This refinement and development likewise continue as long as the individual continues to learn. The newer demands made on reading by the secondary school curriculum make it unreasonable to expect the elementary school to complete the developmental process.

According to this plan, reading was to be taught to all students in secondary grades just as it was taught to all students in elementary grades. This concept still holds true in the present use of the term *developmental reading*.

More recently the term *corrective reading* has come into use. This is the type of reading with which this book deals, and it probably is the kind that does "the greatest good for the greatest number."

Distinctions will now be made between *remedial reading* and *corrective reading*. According to the writer's interpretation, the difference between these two kinds of reading resides in the degree of intensity and complexity of the problem. With this concept in view, more specific differences will be pointed out.

The term *remedial reading* at present is commonly applied to work with those students who are seriously retarded in reading, and who need highly specialized diagnosis and intensive treatment. Often these students are taught individually, sometimes in small groups, each of which is made up of students having the same type of difficulties, who are reading at about the same instructional level and who require similar treatment in reading. Contemporaneously, some of these cases may be receiving treatment for other difficulties from specialists in other fields. It often takes a comparatively long period of treatment for such students to reach their mental potential in reading achievement.

Corrective reading has been defined carefully in Dr. Robinson's discussion in the second chapter of this book. Briefly, however, in answer to an administrator's question, a short statement such as the following might be made: *Corrective reading* is used to designate the type of work done with less serious cases, those who perhaps are retarded only a year or so in terms of potential, who apparently have no deep-seated causes of difficulty, and who respond readily to treatment. Such students usually are taught in groups according to their particular needs and ability.

Power reading is the latest term to become popular. *Power reading* is similar to *developmental reading* except that in this type of reading the student is supposed to achieve a power in speed and comprehension far above that normally expected at his grade level. For example, one super-intendent reported that in the preceding year 40 per cent of his graduates were accepted at Harvard. These students had been high achievers and excellent readers. After they had entered Harvard, the superintendent sent the students a questionnaire asking if the secondary school could have done any more than it did to prepare them for their study at Harvard. Several replied "Yes, you could have given us some reading courses in our senior year." These students wanted *power reading*.

How Can We Convince Parents and Students That Corrective Reading Is Necessary?

"My students and their parents have reached the point of accepting remedial instruction for serious retardation in reading, but if I start talking about teaching corrective reading in classrooms I meet with resistance," said Mr. Parks. "They think it is a waste of time for students, who in their opinion are already reading fairly well, to have reading instruction when they should be concentrating on their high school subjects."

In situations such as Mr. Parks describes, it is helpful to respond readily with some of the reasons why we should teach not only corrective reading but also developmental reading and even power reading in secondary schools. A few such considerations follow.

1. Perhaps the most important reason springs from the job situation. Due to the technological revolution there will be a drastic decrease in the need for unskilled labor. More education will be necessary in obtaining and holding jobs in the future and good reading ability is necessary in obtaining such an education. Because of concern for the job problem, secondary schools are urged to provide effective reading instruction for all students who would profit by it, and if needed, to continue to provide such instruction all through the secondary grades. Being able to read well is necessary in earning a livelihood.

2. Another reason, in addition to the job situation, also arises from our modern civilization. It is based on the fact that our present fast-moving age demands of everyone a faster and more effective type of reading. Never before have there been so many urgent challenges for

reading, never has there been such a diversity of reading materials, and never has there been so little time in which to read. The complexity of the space age requires a better reading public than we have ever had. It is of crucial importance that we turn out students equipped to meet the new reading demands of our contemporary life.

3. Another reason why we should teach reading at higher levels, and a fortunate one in terms of the needs expressed above, is that reading skills lend themselves to continuity of growth. All of us probably could read more rapidly than we do. All of us probably could read with greater depths of understanding. It is possible to continue to grow in reading all through secondary school and college, and all through life. Why stop cultivating reading growth at the end of the sixth grade? Let us help students continue to grow.

4. Further, surveys throughout the country reveal that thousands of high school students are not reading as well as they should. If students haven't acquired adequate skills to handle their reading needs at any level in high school, then it is none too soon for secondary teachers to begin corrective reading at that point, in order that this reading lag may be caught up as soon as possible.

In addition to giving sound reasons to students and parents, the guidance counselor can serve as a key person in convincing both parties of the reading needs of certain individuals by discussing with them scores made on reading tests and comparing these with standard norms. Other informative measures may be taken such as sending home bulletins, pamphlets, or school newspapers dealing with the desirability of teaching reading at secondary level and inviting a reading specialist or someone from a school that has a successful reading program to talk at an assembly or at a parents' meeting.

How Can We Better Involve Subject Matter Teachers in a Corrective Reading Program?

The above question is one which is frequently asked by administrators. The situation, described by Mr. Fisher, is typical: "We got along fine in the old routine in which the reading teacher took a small number of seriously retarded readers for remedial work. She was specialized in that area and everyone was willing to let her do the job. But, eventually, the idea of corrective reading came up. This would involve a much larger number of students. At this point, it was suggested that teachers in the content areas do some teaching of reading. Then the real controversy began! Should subject teachers become involved in the reading program? If so, how can this be done?"

Content area teachers should be present at all preliminary activities designed to stimulate interest in a school reading program, including discussion of the school's test results in reading, talks by a reading specialist, review and discussion of recent articles or books on teaching reading at secondary level, and visitation to other schools that already have a successful reading program.

During these preliminary activities, two facts should become clearly apparent: (1) While a certain body of common skills is used in all subject areas, there are specific skills needed in reading in different content fields; (2) Efforts of all teachers are needed in effecting reading improvement in the school as a whole.

The responsibility of the subject teachers in regard to these skills should be made clear. This responsibility is two-fold: (1) If a reading teacher or an English teacher is teaching basic reading skills, it is the responsibility of subject teachers to become acquainted with his activities so that applications of general skills may be made in their special fields; (2) A second responsibility of subject teachers is that of teaching specific reading skills needed in their respective content areas.

After preliminaries are over and it is time actually to sketch out a program for the school under consideration, subject teachers should become personally involved in all of the planning activities. It has been found helpful to have the teachers in each subject area constitute a committee, with the head of the department serving as chairman. These small groups then hold series of meetings in which they discuss the special reading needs of students in their respective fields, and eventually make a report at a faculty meeting. Decisions can then be made as to those skills to be emphasized by the teacher responsible for teaching reading, and those which should receive special attention in certain subject fields.

Proceeding thus far is good, but another step must be taken. The subject teacher will want to know *how* he can apply skills taught by the teacher of reading and *how* to teach special skills needed in his particular field. As a means of meeting these needs, the committees may meet again to formulate their questions in regard to aspects of teaching reading with which they would like assistance. At this point, the subject teachers should have an opportunity to consult with a trained reading specialist in their school system or from another school or university. It is also helpful if they may be given an in-service course by a person competent to offer them the services which they are seeking.

What Are Some Specific Things Subject Teachers Can Do in Their Own Classrooms?

Chapters five through nine in this book provide excellent answers to this question. The busy administrator, however, wants short and specific answers. To him, in the interest of brevity, perhaps two or three examples might be given of situations in which subject teachers have taught corrective reading in response to needs of their students.

A social studies teacher decided to teach by the unit method. He chose his unit topics carefully, planned lectures to stimulate interest in each topic and prepared appropriate reference lists. At the beginning of the semester he gave a lecture to build background for a certain topic. As an assignment the students were asked to find additional information on different aspects of this topic. When they came to class next day they had practically nothing to offer. The teacher gave them the same assignment again and told them emphatically to come back the following day with information to contribute to discussion of the topic. Again they came to class with practically nothing in the way of additional information. The teacher reproached them and told them to get busy and find the required information. On the third day they were no more responsive than on the two preceding days.

In the meantime the teacher had discovered that these students didn't know how to find the information necessary to implement their study of the unit. Being an astute teacher, he used his social studies period for an entire week in teaching his students the location skills necessary in searching for the required information. From this time on, things ran smoothly and the students carried out their assignments as expected. This teacher was teaching corrective reading. He was supplying reading skills that were lacking. He was meeting a need in one of his classes which would enable his students to work more effectively in studying their particular subject.

A science teacher complained. "Most of my students do not distinguish between minor details and important statements. They respond with insignificant little bits instead of significant points. Is there anything that I, as a science teacher, can do about this?"

This teacher was advised by a reading specialist to teach his students to find the main idea, major details and minor details in paragraphs using science materials, and he was shown methods of doing this. For several days, considerable time was devoted to teaching this technique using the students' textbook in science. Later in the year, this teacher reported marked improvement in his students' ability to sort the important from the unimportant in their reading of science.

A mathematics teacher identified a reading need of his students in this way: "In reading problems a great many students skip over the prepositions, conjunctions, and adverbial and prepositional phrases. Such words and phrases as *to, from, by, larger than, part of* receive no attention from them even though such words and phrases are very important in ascertaining relationships among the numbers in problems, and are important in following directions for working problems. The student's attention seems to be directed exclusively to image words and numbers. He reads just those words which appeal to his eye and omits the rest of the sentence. As a result, problems are worked out on the basis of his own imagination and its play on the numbers, not according to the facts as presented in the problems.

This teacher corrected this deficiency by devoting a few minutes at the end of each period to the oral reading of some of the problems in the next assignment. During this oral reading, students were held to absolute accuracy in reading the kinds of words and phrases enumerated above, and the importance of these words and phrases was discussed thoroughly. Later, the students were given practice in reading silently and telling which of the smaller words or phrases were important in solving each of several problems and why. Using this approach, the reading difficulty in math was corrected.

If the administrator will read chapters five through nine he will find a multitude of other ways in which subject teachers can teach corrective reading. In the meantime, perhaps the above examples will point to possibilities.

Where Can I Get a Qualified Reading Specialist?

"I want a fully-qualified, experienced reading specialist, not just a remedial reading teacher. Our school needs someone who has specialized not only in remedial reading but who thoroughly understands corrective reading and developmental reading at secondary levels. Such a person is very hard to find. Where shall I look?"

This problem is a common one among administrators who employ reading personnel. It is true that there is a definite shortage of qualified specialists at the present time, particularly those who are experienced in teaching reading at secondary level and who have had reading courses specially designed for this level, as well as for the elementary level. As a result of the present interest in reading at higher academic levels many colleges and universities are adding courses in secondary reading, and increasing numbers of teachers are preparing themselves to be specialists at this level. So the shortage in specialists should become less acute in the future.

At the present time the best answer to the question, "Where can I find a reading specialist?" is: go to the teacher placement bureau of a college or university in your own or a neighboring state, one that offers a strong reading specialization program that includes one or more courses in the teaching of reading in secondary schools. If this placement bureau has no one available, try others in neighboring colleges or universities. If you live in a state that is particularly attractive to teachers, you might write to educational institutions in other states, especially those that are known to have excellent programs for the preparation of reading specialists. Make your contacts as early as February or March because good reading specialists are in strong demand.

If you are unsuccessful in obtaining a qualified specialist from a college or university placement bureau, the next possibility is to develop a reading specialist of your own. Select one of your teachers who is deeply interested in reading, preferably one who has taught reading successfully and demonstrated his or her ability to get along well with other teachers, parents, and children. Suggest that this person begin taking courses in preparation for serving as a reading consultant in your system. If the selected person is unable to take a leave-of-absence for study, then evening, Saturday, and summer session courses may serve the purpose.

What Should I Look for in Employing a Reading Specialist?

1. Motive for specialization in reading. Is the person genuinely interested in this field, or does he want to be a reading specialist because he thinks this will be an easier job than teaching in a regular classroom?

2. Undergraduate and graduate training. Does this person have a master's degree with specialization in reading? (Some have a doctor's degree which is better yet, but a master's is essential.)

3. Specialization in reading. Where did he have specialized preparation in reading? Has he taken several courses in reading including a basic methods course, reading diagnosis, remedial and corrective reading,

reading at the secondary level, laboratory practicum, supervision of reading?

4. Courses in related areas. Has he taken courses related to special work in reading such as measurement and evaluation, mental hygiene, educational psychology, child or adolescent psychology, children's literature, and other related fields.

5. Experience. Has the applicant had experience in teaching developmental reading? Corrective reading? Remedial reading? At what levels? With what success?

6. Does this person get along well with other teachers? Students? Parents?

What May I Expect of a Reading Consultant in Secondary School?

Some administrators are not sure of the role which a reading consultant should have in the total administrative set-up, or of the duties which he should expect of this member of his staff.

In response to inquiries about this matter, it might be stated that the reading consultant should be an auxiliary to the administrative staff, serving in the same general capacity as a librarian, guidance counselor, nurse, etc., and he needs to work closely with other auxiliary personnel. While he does not have administrative power, his position is one of primary importance. His major role is two-fold: to serve as an interpreter and as a skill developer. He needs to interpret reading objectives, skills, methods, and needs to teachers, principals, children, parents, and higher administrative officers if they desire such information. As skill developer he teaches remedial, corrective, or developmental reading in keeping with the overall policy of the school.

Surveys have revealed the following duties as among those that reading consultants most frequently perform at the secondary level: they teach reading to students, serve as a consultant to teachers of English, serve as a consultant to subject teachers, conduct demonstration lessons, help teachers select reading materials, supervise the teaching of reading, hold conferences with parents, give talks to community groups, and conduct in-service courses in reading.

Would You Suggest a Few Pointers on Starting a Reading Program?

The above question is often asked by administrators who have not as yet done anything about initiating reading programs in their secondary schools, or who have limited programs, perhaps having only remedial reading taught to a few students. These administrators want suggestions in regard to definite steps that they can take in starting or extending a reading program. In answer to this request, these suggestions are given:

1. The administrator should have some background in reading gained through attending meetings and conferences dealing with secondary reading, and as a result of his own reading of recent books and articles on this subject.

2. The administrator should be enthusiastic about starting a reading program and confident of its success. He should talke leadership in providing interest-stimulating activities such as those suggested in the appendix to this book.

3. The administrator should make budgetary provisions for purchasing extra reading materials.

4. The administrator should schedule time for teaching reading except in schools where team-teaching is being used. In such schools teams of teachers schedule the time with the approval of the administrator.

5. Support of the entire staff should be enlisted.

6. Support of the students and their parents should be obtained.

7. The undertaking should be a cooperative one in which all members of the faculty participate in planning the program from the beginning.

8. While the plan is cooperative, the responsibility for developing the program should be given to one person: the reading specialist, principal, curriculum director, classroom teacher, or someone else who is interested and competent.

9. The person to whom the above responsibility is given *must* be trained in reading.

10. When ready to start the program, care should be taken to make sure that each person involved knows what his responsibility is.

11. The administrator must be ready to accept small beginnings. A well-rounded reading program takes time to develop. The administrator needs to keep enthusiasm at a high ebb, but he often will find it necessary to temper enthusiasm with patience.

What About In-Service Courses?

"I am planning to have some in-service courses in reading for our teachers. Any suggestions about the content and organization of such courses?" This quotation is typical. There is a growing need for in-service courses in secondary reading and the administrator's questions about such courses are frequently heard.

Perhaps, the first and most important point that can be made in answer to such questions is this: be sure your teachers are ready for such a course before you make arrangements to have one given. The contrasting examples that follow will emphasize the significance of this advice.

Superintendent *A* decided that it was time to initiate a reading program in the secondary school. He announced his intention at a teachers' meeting, and said that he was planning to have an in-service course given. He stated that all teachers in all subjects were to take the course and that their tuition would be paid from school funds.

The superintendent then employed a professor in a neighboring university to come to the school to give the course. It began on the following Tuesday night. The teachers arrived grudgingly and unhappily, giving expression to such complaints as these: they had enough to do without teaching another subject; reading belonged in the elementary grades anyhow; if teachers were required to take a course it should be one in a subject in which they were interested; some teachers said they had other appointments on Tuesday nights and being asked to take this course interfered with their personal lives; and so on.

Attitudes changed but little throughout the course and at the end the professor, who had conducted the course, felt that it had been of little value to those who had taken it. The last news from this high school was that most of the secondary teachers were still resisting the innovation of teaching reading in their school.

Superintendent *B* in another town was eager to have a comprehensive reading program in his secondary school. As a first step he had reading tests given to all high school students at the end of September. The guidance counselor presented the results at a faculty meeting. The school was far below the national norms. Teachers were given scores of their individual students. Many of these students were two, three, or more grades below expectations. Excitement was high. "What can we do about it?" the teachers asked. "This is a serious matter," replied the superintendent. "Think about it. Talk it over among yourselves. Next week we'll meet and discuss your suggestions."

One of the suggestions offered at the next meeting, and voted on unanimously, was to "Get someone out here to give us a course in reading." Together the teachers selected the college professor they wanted to give the course, and arranged a suitable time and day of the week for it was to be scheduled. In this case, it will be noted that the teachers were involved in the entire plan from the beginning.

The course was attended by a large number of teachers even though their attendance was voluntary. Morale was high, discussion was abundant, and study was earnest. Out of the course grew plans for another course in which teachers of different subjects were to meet in committees, in attempts to discover the reading skills needed in their respective subject fields, after which the instructor would be asked for help in meeting these needs. Another result of this course was the formulation by the teachers of a plan to prepare a course of study in reading for their school.

The implication, which the above illustrations is intended to convey, is that something should be done to establish readiness for an in-service reading course if it is to serve its purpose fully. The superintendent in the second example used the results of a school-wide standardized reading test as an initial step. There are other interest-stimulating activities, used singly or in combination, which may result in a desire on the part of teachers to have an in-service course in reading.

1. The superintendent may discuss the trend toward having all teachers teach reading in high school; describe situations in which this has been done, and make available to his teachers articles and books describing the experiences of others in instituting all-school reading programs.

2. At faculty meetings subject teachers may give five-minute reports of articles on secondary reading which have appeared in current periodicals, or reports on different chapters in recent books dealing with this subject.

3. It may be suggested that each teacher give an informal three-minute, ten-question test to his students based on a textbook used in his field. Each student may count the number of words he reads and attempt to answer the ten questions the teacher has prepared. A comparison, by the teacher, of speed and comprehension scores made by different students in the same class will be revealing. It is especially helpful if teachers of different subjects give such informal tests using a textbook in their respective fields. A study of scores made in different subject areas by the same students may lead to very worthwhile observations.

4. Arrangements may be made for teachers to pay a few visits to classrooms to observe the procedures of elementary teachers in developing some of the different reading skills. Such visits often aid secondary teachers in becoming more skill conscious.

5. In discussing ways of convincing parents and students of the need for reading in secondary school, it was suggested in an earlier chapter

that qualified speakers be brought in. This same plan is useful in developing readiness in teachers for training.

Through such experiences as those mentioned above, secondary teachers become aware of the need for teaching reading and develop a greater sensitivity to needs in their own school. If such activities are skillfully executed by the administrator, teachers are likely to become so interested that they will not only desire, but perhaps request, an in-service course.

As for the nature and content of in-service courses in secondary reading, these are matters that should be considered carefully when the administrator is making arrangements for the course or courses. Some suggestions in regard to nature and content are offered below.

It is possible to have the first in-service course offered without bringing in an outside instructor. Some secondary schools start out by arranging for a series of demonstrations given by elementary teachers. The series must be well-planned in terms of requests made by the secondary teachers and the desirability of showing as many different reading skills as possible. If the school system has a reading consultant at the elementary level, this consultant can be helpful in planning the demonstrations but the secondary teachers should have a strong part in the planning.

When the time comes to engage an outside reading specialist to give one or more in-service courses, the administrator should plan carefully with this person. If a reading teacher or English teacher is already teaching reading in the secondary school, then he also should have conferences with the person who is to give the course. Through such conferences, the instructor will gain significant insights into the school situation in which he will be working.

The first in-service course given by an outside specialist should be highly practical. The instructor should be expected to respect the requests of the class. At the same time he should be given leeway to supplement teacher requests. This is necessary in order that a complete overview of the skills program in reading may be presented and in order that a variety of methods may be given for teaching these skills, both at elementary and secondary levels. Acquainting the teachers in the class with the many instructional materials available for use with secondary students also is a "must" for any in-service course.

Other in-service courses may deal with the possibilities of corrective work and the teaching of specialized reading skills needed in working in the different subject areas. In such a course, teachers may work in committees organized in terms of their special subjects as previously mentioned in the earlier discussion of involvement of subject-matter teachers. The major activities of an in-service course of this type should be concerned with teacher thinking, creativity, planning, and leadership. On the other hand the guidance and counsel of a highly competent reading specialist is needed. Courses of this type may well, and often do, lead into the preparation by the staff members of a course of study in reading for their own secondary school.

Summary

This chapter has discussed certain recurring questions which school administrators are asking about the teaching of reading in the secondary school. The questions were concerned with the following topics: defining terms used to designate different kinds of reading instruction, convincing parents and students of the need for reading instruction, involving subject matter teachers in a reading program, giving specific examples of corrective reading in classrooms of subject matter teachers, stating qualifications of a reading consultant, explaining the place and function of a reading consultant in the total operation of a school, giving some pointers in regard to starting a reading program, and implementing in-service courses.

The teaching of reading at the secondary level is a fast-moving, rapidly changing and significant aspect of education. In order that the administrator and his staff may benefit continuously from fresh information about reading instruction, it is recommended that he make an effort to keep the school library well-stocked with recent professional books, pamphlets, and periodicals on this subject. His responsibility will not end, however, when he has supplied these professional materials. If the materials are used effectively it will be necessary for him to generate warm, contagious enthusiasm which, he, himself, has derived from reading some of these professional materials. The results would be rewarding for him, his teachers and his students.

In conclusion, I should like to present a quotation. Coleridge, the English poet, did a very good informal reading diagnosis many years ago when he wrote:

There are four kinds of readers. The first is like an hour-glass; and their reading being as the sand, it runs out, and leaves not a vestige behind. A second is like the sponge, which imbibes everything and returns it in nearly the same state, only a little dirtier. The third is like a jelly-bag, allowing all that is pure to pass away, and retaining only the refuse and dregs. And the fourth is like the slaves in the diamond mines of Golconda, who, cast aside all that is worthless, retain only pure gems.

Perhaps when all the reading questions of administrators are answered satisfactorily, and all secondary teachers are teaching corrective reading effectively, we shall be able to develop a race of individuals who will "cast aside all that is worthless," and who will "retain only pure gems."

REFERENCES

1. Anderson, C. J. and Merton, E. "Remedial Work on Reading," *Elementary School Journal*, XXI (January 1921), 336-348.
2. Bond, Guy L. and Bond, Eva. *Developmental Reading in High School*. New York: Macmillan, 1941, p. 54.
3. Gray, W. S. and Others. *Remedial Cases in Reading: Their Diagnosis and Treatment*, Supplemental Educational Monographs. Chicago: University of Chicago Press, 1922.
4. Smith, Nila Banton. *American Reading Instruction*. Newark, Delaware: International Reading Association, 1965, pp. 155-156, 189-190.
5. Uhl, W. L. "The Use of the Results of Tests as a Basis for Planning Remedial Work," *Elementary School Journal*, XVII (January 1921), 273-280.

APPENDIX

ADELINE PRENER

Memorial Junior High School
Valley Stream, New York

A. SELECTED REFERENCES FOR THE CLASSROOM TEACHER

Bamman, Henry A.; Hogan, Ursula; and Greene, Charles E. *Reading Instruction in the Secondary School*. New York: Longmans, Green and Company, 1961.

Bond, Guy L. and Bond, Eva. *Developmental Reading in High School*. New York: The Macmillan Company, 1941, Chap. 7, 8.

Bond, Guy L. and Handlan, Bertha. *Adapting Instruction in Reading to Individual Differences*, Series on Individualization of Instruction, No. 5. Minneapolis: University of Minnesota Press, 1948.

Brueckner, Leo J. and Bond, Guy L. *The Diagnosis and Treatment of Learning Difficulties*. New York: Appleton-Century-Crofts, Inc., 1955, Chap. 8, 9.

Dawson, Mildred A. and Bamman, Henry A. *Fundamentals of Basic Reading Instruction, Second Edition*. New York: David McKay Co., 1963, Chap. 14, 15.

DeBoer, John J. and Whipple, Gertrude. "Reading Development in Other Curriculum Areas," Chapter IV, *Development In and Through Reading*, 60th Yearbook of the National Society for the Study of Education. Chicago: University of Chicago Press, 1961.

Deighton, Lee C. *Vocabulary Development in the Classroom*. New York: Bureau of Publications, Teachers College, Columbia University, 1959.

Fay, Leo (and discussants Mallinson, George G. and Bracken, Dorothy Kendall). "Responsibility for and Methods of Promoting Growth in Reading in Content Areas," *Better Readers for Our Times*, International Reading Association Conference Proceedings, Vol. 1, pp. 88-95. New York: Scholastic Magazines, 1956.

Fay, Leo. *What Research Says to the Teacher: Reading in the High School*. Washington, D. C.: Dep't of Classroom Teachers and American Educational Research Association of the NEA, 1956.

130

Gray, William S. (Ed.). *Improving Reading in Content Fields,* Supplementary Educational Monographs, No. 62. Chicago: The University of Chicago Press, January, 1947.

Gray, William S. (Ed.). *Classroom Techniques in Improving Reading,* Supplementary Educational Monographs, No. 69. Chicago: The University of Chicago Press, October, 1949.

Gray, William S. (Ed.). *Improving Reading in All Curriculum Areas,* Supplementary Educational Monographs, No. 76. Chicago: The University of Chicago Press, 1952.

Harris, Albert J. *How to Increase Reading Ability, Fourth Edition.* New York: David McKay Company, 1961, Chap. 15, 16.

Haugh, Oscar M. (Ed.). *Teaching Reading in High School,* Kansas Studies in Education, Vol. 10, No. 1. Lawrence, Kansas: University of Kansas Press, February, 1960.

Heilman, Arthur W. *Principles and Practices of Teaching Reading.* Columbus, Ohio: Charles E. Merrill Books, Inc., 1961, Chap. 8, 9.

Janes, Edith. "Assessing the Reading Needs of Students in the Content Areas," *Reading as an Intellectual Activity,* International Reading Association Conference Proceedings, Vol. 8, pp. 97-99. New York: Scholastic Magazines, 1963.

Jewett, Arno (Ed.). *Improving Reading in the Junior High School,* Bulletin No. 10, U. S. Department of Health, Education, and Welfare. Washington, D. C.: Government Printing Office, 1957, pp. 71-97.

Kottmeyer, William. *Handbook for Remedial Reading.* St. Louis, Webster, 1959, Chap. 7, 8.

Lazar, May (Ed.). *The Retarded Reader in the Junior High School; A Guide for Supervisors and Teachers.* New York: Board of Education of the City of New York, 1952, Chap. 11-14.

National Association of Secondary School Principals. *Improving Reading Instruction in the Secondary School* (Bulletin, N.A.S.S.P.). Washington, D. C.: National Association of Secondary School Principals, 1950.

National Society for the Study of Education. *Reading in the High School and College,* 47th Yearbook, Part II. Chicago: The University of Chicago Press, 1948, Chap. 7, 8.

Niles, Olive S. "How Much Does a Content Teacher Need to Know about Methods of Teaching Reading?" *Improvement of Reading through Classroom Practice,* IRA Conference Proceedings IX, pp.

41-42. Newark, Delaware: International Reading Association, 1964.

Reading, Grades 7, 8, 9: A Teacher's Guide to Curriculum Planning, Curriculum Bulletin No. 11, 1957-58 Series. New York: Board of Education of the City of New York, 1959.

Reading in Secondary Schools, Bulletin of the Bureau of Secondary Curriculum Development. Albany, New York: The State Education Department, 1965, pp. 30-53.

Reading in the Subject Areas, Grades 7, 8, 9, Curriculum Bulletin No. 6, 1963-64 Series. New York: Board of Education of the City of New York, 1964.

The Reading Teacher, September, 1961 and September, 1963. Newark, Delaware: International Reading Association.

Robinson, H. Alan and Rauch, Sidney J. *Guiding the Reading Program.* Chicago: Science Research Associates, 1965, Chap. 5, 6.

Robinson, H. Alan. "Teaching Reading in the Content Areas: Some Basic Principles of Instruction," *Improvement of Reading through Classroom Practice,* IRA Conference Proceedings IX, pp. 35-36. Newark, Delaware: International Reading Association, 1964.

Robinson, Helen M. *Why Pupils Fail in Reading.* Chicago: University of Chicago Press, 1945, Chap. 12.

Robinson, Helen M. (Ed.). *Corrective Reading in Classroom and Clinic.* Chicago: University of Chicago Press, 1953.

Sheldon, William D. "Reading Instruction in Junior High School," Chapter XVII, *Development In and Through Reading,* 60th Yearbook of the National Society for the Study of Education. Chicago: University of Chicago Press, 1961.

Smith, Nila Banton. *Be a Better Reader* Series, Books I-VI. Englewood Cliffs, New Jersey: Prentice-Hall, 1959.

Smith, Nila Banton. "Patterns of Writing in Different Subject Areas," *Journal of Reading,* Vol. VIII, No. 1 and No. 2 (October 1964, November, 1964), pp. 31-39, 97-102.

Smith, Nila Banton. *Reading Instruction for Today's Children.* Englewood Cliffs, New Jersey: Prentice-Hall, 1963, Chap. 10.

Smith, Nila Banton. "Reading in Subject Matter Fields," *Educational Leadership,* Vol. 22, No. 6 (March 1965), pp. 382-385.

Spache, George D. *The Art of Efficient Reading.* New York: The Macmillan Company, 1965.

Spache, George D. "Types and Purposes of Reading in Various Curriculum Fields," *The Reading Teacher,* Vol. 11, No. 3 (February

1958), pp. 158-64.

Stewart, L. Jane; Heller, Frieda M.; and Albert, Elsie J. *Improving Reading in the Junior High School.* New York: Appleton-Century-Crofts, 1957.

Strang, Ruth M. *Reading and the Junior High School Teacher,* Bulletin No. 12. Middletown, Connecticut: Department of School Services and Publications, Wesleyan University, 1959.

Strang, Ruth and Bracken, Dorothy Kendall. *Making Better Readers.* Boston: D. C. Heath and Company, 1957, Chap. 5.

Strang, Ruth; McCullough, Constance; and Traxler, Arthur E. *Problems in the Improvement of Reading.* New York: McGraw-Hill, 1955, Chap. 7-10.

Strang, Ruth; McCullough, Constance M.; and Traxler, Arthur E. *The Improvement of Reading,* 3rd edition. New York: McGraw-Hill, 1961, Chap. 5-8.

Triggs, Frances. *We All Teach Reading.* New York: Frances Triggs, 419 W. 119 Street, New York, New York 10027, 1954.

B. ADDITIONAL REFERENCES FOR SPECIFIC SUBJECT AREAS

Social Studies

Carpenter, Helen McCracken (Editor). *Skill Development in Social Studies,* 33rd Yearbook. Washington, D. C.: National Council for the Social Studies, 1963.

Dallman, Martha E. "Classroom Reading for Social Studies," *The Grade Teacher,* 78 (October 1960), p. 404.

Five Steps to Reading Success in Science, Social Studies, and Mathematics. New York: Metropolitan School Study Council, Teachers College, Columbia University, 1960.

Huus, Helen. "Antidote for Apathy—Acquiring Reading Skills for Social Studies," *Challenge and Experiment in Reading,* International Reading Association Conference Proceedings, Vol. 7, pp. 81-88. New York: Scholastic Magazines, 1962.

McAulay, J. D. "Social Studies Dependent on Reading," *Education,* Vol. 8 (October 1961), pp. 87-89.

Nowell, Lillian. "Developing Concepts in the Social Sciences," *The Reading Teacher,* Vol. 17 (September 1963), pp. 10-15.

Preston, Ralph C.; Schneyer, J. Wesley; and Thyng, Franc J. *Guiding the Social Studies Reading of High School Students,* Bulletin 34. Washington: National Council for the Social Studies, 1963.

Shepherd, David L. *Effective Reading in the Social Studies.* Evanston, Illinois: Row, Peterson and Company, 1961.

Witty, Paul A. "The Role of Reading in the Social Studies," *Elementary English,* XXXIX (October 1962), pp. 562-569.

Science

Brown, Walter R. "Science Textbook Selection and the Dale-Chall Formula," *School Science and Mathematics,* LXV (February 1965), pp. 164-167.

Carter, Homer L. J. "Helping Students to Read Scientific Material," *Reading for Effective Living,* International Reading Association Conference Proceedings, Vol. 3, pp. 174-177. New York: Scholastic Magazines, 1958.

Crombie, Charles W., "Selecting Science Textbooks," *Science Education,* XXXV (December 1951), pp. 276-278.

Deck, Ray F. "Vocabulary Development to Improve Reading and Achievement in Science," *American Biology Teacher,* XIV (January 1952), pp. 13-15.

Five Steps to Reading Success in Science, Social Studies, and Mathematics. New York: Metropolitan School Study Council, Teachers College, Columbia University, 1960.

Mallinson, George G. "Reading Materials for Slow Learners and Readers in Science," *Materials for Reading,* Supplementary Educational Monograph, No. 86. Chicago: University of Chicago Press, December 1957, pp. 151-154.

Mallinson, George G. "Methods and Materials for Teaching Reading in Science," *Sequential Development of Reading Abilities,* Supplementary Educational Monograph, No. 90. Chicago: University of Chicago Press, December 1960, pp. 145-149.

Mallinson, George G. "Reading and the Teaching of Science," *School Science and Mathematics,* LXIV (February 1964), pp. 148-153.

Mallinson, George G. "Reading and the Teaching of Science, Part I," *Current Science-Teacher's Edition,* L (October 5-9, 1964), pp. 1-2.

Mallinson, George G. "Reading and the Teaching of Science, Part II," *Current Science-Teacher's Edition,* L (October 19-23, 1964), pp. 1-3.

Mallinson, George Greisen. "How to Use the Textbook in Science Teaching," *School Science and Mathematics,* LIII (November 1953), pp. 593-600.

Shepherd, David L. "Teaching Science and Mathematics to the Seriously Retarded Reader in the High School," *The Reading Teacher,* Vol. 17 (September 1963), pp. 25-30.

Shepherd, David L. *Effective Reading in Science.* Evanston, Illinois: Row, Peterson and Company, 1960.

Mathematics

Dadourian, H. M. *How to Study How to Solve.* Reading, Massachusetts: Addison-Wesley Publishing Company, 1957.

Five Steps to Reading Success in Science, Social Studies and Mathematics. New York: Metropolitan School Study Council, Teachers College, Columbia University, 1960.

Shepherd, David L. "Teaching Science and Mathematics to the Seriously Retarded Reader in the High School," *The Reading Teacher,* Vol. 17 (September 1963), pp. 25-30.

Hartung, Maurice L. "Methods and Materials for Teaching Reading Mathematics," *Sequential Development of Reading Abilities,* Supplementary Educational Monographs. Chicago: The University of Chicago Press, 1960, pp. 140-144.

Spencer, Peter L., and Russell, David H. "Reading in Arithmetic," (Chapter 9), *Instruction in Arithmetic,* 25th Yearbook. Washington, D. C.: The National Council of Teachers of Mathematics, 1960, pp. 202-223.